CONVERSION
TO THE WORLD

Hans Jürgen Schultz

New York

CHARLES SCRIBNER'S SONS

CONTENTS

AMERICAN FOREWORD

by Harvey Cox

AFTER a period of confusion and uncertainty, the theological conversation in America seems to have divided into two somewhat contrasting schools of thought. The first includes those on both sides of the "problem of God" altercation, *i.e.* the philosophical-"death of God" theologians, Altizer, Hamilton, and their followers, and those who are reviving an interest in the doctrine of God, such as Gilkey, Ogden and others.

Working at a different task are those for whom speculative concern about the existence of God is a subsidiary question. They see "religious" issues as obsolete and wish to extend Bonhoeffer's ideas about a non-religious interpretation into a discussion about how this affects the task of Christianity today. This second school, with which I feel a closer sympathy, includes such people as Leslie Dewart, J. C. Hoekendijk, and Richard Shaull. Hans Jürgen Schultz definitely stands in this *second* category. He includes a chapter on the God problem, but he calls it "The Illusion of a Godless World" and refers in it mainly to Hoekendijk, Bonhoeffer and Simone Weil. For him the God problem is mainly a problem in life and mission, not a speculative query.

1

This book is both readable and radical. In stating his case, Schultz draws on the most seminal thinkers in the modern world and fuses insights that one rarely finds in combination, *i.e.* those of Max Frisch, Teilhard de Chardin, Bert Brecht and Christoph Blumhardt. Since I have admired all these people, but usually with different facets of my mind, I found the mix delightful.

Schultz's thesis is that the presence of God today means openness, relativity, freedom. He makes intelligent use of Friedrich Gogarten's historic theological analysis of secularization. It is good to have some information on Gogarten since he will become an increasingly significant figure on the theological scene as his works begin to appear in English and as we find we must deal with an open-minded theology of history, one that appreciates and understands secularization. This book affirms the worldliness and secularity of our time, but does not surrender to our age's *own understanding* of that secularity. With Gogarten, Schultz sees our modern secular and scientific revolutions as rooted in the preaching of the Gospel in the Western world. He correctly argues that the impact of this Gospel was to "de-religionize" the world itself by proclaiming that only God was holy and therefore the world was *not* divine. This freed the world to be world and therefore freed man to be man.

One of Schultz's most valuable sections is the one he entitles "Experiment in Freedom." In discussing the emerging shape of the modern church he escapes the anti-institutional bias which has characterized so much recent writing on this subject. He calls for the development of cell-type, flexible and mobile groups closely related to the differentiated structures of modern society. He sounds a bit like a German Stephen Rose. But he also sees that the church must continue to be one organization *among* others in addition to being a stimulus to change and self-criticism *within* other organizations. He points out accurately that this double-existence has characterized the church during most of the years of its life.

I believe he is right about this and that his discussion goes beyond the pro-church/anti-church *cul de sac* in which our American debate was once bogged down. We need *various* forms of church life. We need to be a city on a hill *and* the salt of the earth, both gathered and dispersed, both organized to wield power *and* mobile and flexible enough to be present within other institutions.

The idea of a "conversion to the world" did not originate with Schultz. Nor does it come, as some readers might think, from Dietrich Bonhoeffer. The so-called "religious socialists" of the early twentieth century, people like Ragaz and Cuttar, had similar notions. The phrase itself probably originated with the famous father and son Blumhardt team who mixed a form of German pietism with a passionate concern for this world that greatly influenced the religious socialists. Most people know that Tillich was a religious socialist in his youth. Fewer people know that Karl Barth also started out with this group. Although they were lost from sight with the coming of dialectical theology, one finds in many places today a conviction that we are in for a rediscovery and renaissance of the religious socialists. I hope this is true. Our need for a properly framed and theologically well-grounded theology of politics will never be provided by a reductive existentialist theology. Even Sartre, master of the genre, has a hard time squeezing a political ethic out of existentialism. This present book reaches back before the existentialist movement and ahead to the future opening up before us. It speaks for a frankly political style of Christian discipleship.

Not only will Schultz supply needed ammunition to American churchmen in search of a political theology. He will also, I hope, whet our appetites for reading the rising new generation of European theologians who are also moving in the direction of secular theology. The reader who finds Schultz interesting should also be stimulated by the young Roman Catholic theologian from Münster, Johannes Baptiste Metz. His mind should also click when he reads Jürgen Moltmann of Bonn, whose *Theologie der Hoffnung* arises out of a rediscovery of the political implications of eschatology and an encounter with the newer currents of Marxist revisionism. The same reader will be stimulated by Trutz Rendtorff of Hamburg who insists that our discovery of the historically conditioned character of all thinking, theological and otherwise, has made the problems of the church, *i.e.* the Christian's social standpoint in theology, central. Rendtorff further contends that the question of the church, since it has to do with one community within world history, is always a political one. All these thinkers would agree that critical solidarity with the world is the way the church exhibits and proclaims the Gospel today.

These young European theologians could in some measure be grouped as the "worldly thinkers," as opposed to the others who, regardless of their allegedly radical position, still busy themselves with "religious" questions. There is a parallel in nineteenth-century philosophy. Karl Marx, though an avid atheist in his early years, soon tired of arguing about God and decided that the question would only be settled when the social deformation giving rise to the idea of God was corrected. Other philosophers had talked about the world, he said, but now the time had come to change it. *Conversion to the World* is not a Marxist book, but it does breathe some of its same conviction. The theological questions which pester us today will not be settled by talking about them some more. New insights will arise from action. The church will be granted a message for the world only when it takes that world with unconditional seriousness. Conversion to the world must precede the reappearance of the lost, strayed, stolen or dead God about whom we have recently heard so much. Let us hope that this book helps push American theology out of its sacral ghetto and into God's world.

INTRODUCTION

by Paul Oestreicher

IT IS no part of a translator's task to pre-digest his author's work. Translation itself is inevitably a work of interpretation, as every biblical translator knows. St Paul might well say of many a modern version of his letters: interesting, but not what I wrote. Hans Jürgen Schultz, often just as complex as St Paul, might well, if he reads this translation, fail to recognize parts of his own work. That is a translator's risk and one, in this case, well worth taking. There are complexities, but the central thesis running through this book is as unambiguous as the title itself.

The book, as is proper, speaks for itself. In introducing it I am concerned only incidentally with what it says. My immediate interest is with its context, with the so-called 'new theology' of which it is undoubtedly part.

Most important: Hans Jürgen Schultz is not a theologian. In the German setting that is crucial. He is a layman, 'lay' as opposed to 'ordained'. But in a much more real sense he is anything but a layman: he is a journalist and publicist professionally concerned with communicating the Christian faith to ordinary people. As head of the religious department of South German

7

Radio, Stuttgart—and in many other 'lay' capacities—his reputation in Germany is unrivalled. He is well trained in the intellectual traditions of German protestantism and adds to this a knowledge of philosophy and literature which the German professional theologians generally disdain as irrelevant.

The author makes few concessions to the intellectually lazy. Some readers, as in the case of *Honest to God*, may well ask: 'What's he on about?'. A more significant number, particularly as the author is German, will be grateful that all the things that really matter can be said in the compass of a few pages without a theological 'apparatus' that almost totally obscures every essential. Here is a straightforward plea for the Church's conversion to the world. Here is an attempt to talk in practical terms about the meaning of 'religionless Christianity', without writing one more long speculative treatise on what Dietrich Bonhoeffer might have meant by that term.

This, then, is no theological brain-teaser. The pundits may dismiss it as light-weight. That is the measure of its considerable merit.

*   *   *

In its structures, attitudes and institutions, the Church in Germany is much more thoroughly conservative than anything the Anglo-Saxon world is used to. Perhaps this is surprising to those who see Germany as the seed-bed of nearly all Christian radicalism. It is true that some few eminent theologians have shaken the pillars of the

Church, but so far very few people have bothered to translate theory into practice. There is a deep chasm between the universities and the local church. German protestant preaching of the Word, taken with deadly seriousness, is a strictly disciplined intellectual exercise, academic and remote. Its purity and 'correctness' is unrivalled. Its shape is almost as strictly determined as that of a Japanese no-play. If it does not measure up exegetically and structurally it is by definition a non-sermon. In most cases its power to communicate the relevance of the Gospel to real life is not much greater than that of an Orthodox icon. The effect of an icon on the worshipping *person* is probably much greater.

Traditionally, the Church in a Lutheran or Reformed context has communicated almost only through the Word. The result, paradoxically, has largely been a Church without communication. Theology has been left high and dry. For that reason those few who are determined to break through the communication barrier have often thought it necessary to use battering rams. The theologians have often chosen terminology which has had to shock. They have said many things which, if rightly understood, would not cause a ripple in any British or American congregation. They sound much more revolutionary than they really are. In fact they are merely trying to break icons—and bad ones at that. It is ironical that a theology of the Word should *almost* have led to the breakdown of human communication.

I say *almost*, because the Holy Spirit has never allowed

that to happen. And by the Holy Spirit I mean God speaking through the world. Secular events, political catastrophes, have enabled at least some German Christians over the last forty years or so to come to grips with realities and to respond to them in faith. These events are well known. First there was pagan Nazism to contend with. Then war and near total destruction. Then national division and a cold civil war that still persists. A few German Christians have responded. Many others have used religion as an escape mechanism of one sort or another. This escape has not been utilized only by the pietist anti-intellectuals whose hope is for pie in the sky and whose view of the world is implicitly reactionary. There are also the theological escapists, the intellectual speculators who are so busy asking questions to which no one wants to know the answers—including themselves—that there is no time for living and, in any case, no firm foundations on which to live. And these are most certainly not confined to Germany. Nor are they easy to distinguish from those genuine Christian agnostics who really do want answers. I would not dare to set myself up as judge of who's who in this theological maze.

The father of the modern *iconography of the Word* is indisputably Karl Barth. The complexity of this whole subject immediately becomes evident when his name is mentioned. As both catholic and protestant theologians agree, he is *the* systematic theologian of our century, a modern Aquinas. Perhaps the last. His effect has been strangely contradictory. Of himself, with a profoundly healthy sense of humour, he says 'I am no Barthian'—

and means it. But then there are Barthians and Barthians. Perhaps there is nothing more relevant to this
discussion than Albert Schweitzer writing about Barth
in *The Christian Century*: 'In recent times a tendency has
appeared in dogmatic religion which . . . declares that
religion has nothing to do with the world and civilization. It is not its business to realize the Kingdom of God
on earth. This extreme tendency is mainly represented
by Karl Barth . . . He says a religious person does not
concern himself with what happens to the world . . . All
that concerns the world is the preaching of revealed
truth. Religion is turned aside from the world . . . and in
so doing expresses what the spirit of the age is feeling.'

Fascinating! Schweitzer accusing Barth, of all people,
of selling out the faith to the *Zeitgeist*, to what is popular.
Exactly what those who now preach the 'secular Gospel'
are in their turn being accused of. But Barth belies this
critique in his personal witness. Barth began fairly early
to preach the Gospel politically. Hitler expelled him
from his German university post. His genuine friends
today constitute the German Church's political left.
While the radical demythologizers enjoy their ivory
tower religion, Barth's pupils care about hunger and the
bomb and the challenge of communism. And the
prophet himself preaches in simple meaningful terms to
the prisoners of Basel prison.

There is a happy story about Karl Barth and Martin
Niemöller, through many years the closest of friends. 'It
is amazing,' said the theologian to the political pastor,
'how you always come up with the right answers despite

your lack of theology.' 'On the contrary,' replied Niemöller, 'it is amazing how *you* always come up with the right answer despite all your theology.'

This illustrates nothing more than that there are varied paths to Christian obedience. The essential point, however, is that this obedience can only be measured by its commitment to the world. Barth and Niemöller, the latter more obviously, have been far too busy in the secular world, living the Gospel as they understand it, to preach the 'end of religion'. Anyway, they are both far too 'religious' to be in a position to.

What, in this context, is even more significant is that Dietrich Bonhoeffer was even more deeply religious than either of them, religious in the most obvious sense of that word. Not only was he a highly skilled theologian, but he was a man of deep piety. And not just the early Bonhoeffer who wrote *The Cost of Discipleship* but the political plotter whose prison poems and biblical meditations convey a profound and simple faith. They are psalms of joy and of trusting suffering, they are expressions of hope against hope. They demonstrate the nearness of a very real God.

Yet this same man spoke of the need for 'religionless Christianity'—and was right. He knew the Church too well and loved the world too much not to know that man must outgrow his religious dependence and *be himself* in order to serve men in their real needs. He knew the sociological effect of religion. It had not been a good one and few men had transcended it to assert their humanity. Religion was a luxury the world could ill

afford. Religious man must undergo a second conversion *to the world.*

Religion to Bonhoeffer was not to be confused with
faith. Religion is what he observed in the Church: an
escape into cultic obscurantism. It had to be con-
demned, however uncomfortable. Religion had to do
with saving souls; definitely not man's business. Faith in
Christ was about loving men; man's only business.
Bonhoeffer's ultimate love found its expression in the
dubious role of being party to an (unsuccessful) political
assassination. He was committed to loving action, however paradoxical. And he was prepared to be wrong
because he believed in the forgiveness of sins.

Hans Jürgen Schultz is concerned with man's second
conversion. He is concerned with our love for the world.
And that means involvement and commitment. In a way
it is all as simple as Jesus' saying: 'Not every one who
says to me Lord, Lord, shall enter into the Kingdom,
but he who *does* the will of my Father.' And what is that
will? In one of his better moments St Augustine saw
exactly what it was: *Love, and do what you like!* That is
what St Augustine wrote and not what he is often
quoted as writing: 'Love *God*, and do as you like.' That
is what many Christians would like him to have said.
He did not.

To love must mean to love our fellow men. To love
the world. 'If you do not love your brother whom you
have seen, how can you love God whom you have not
seen?' The Church has shied from the implications of
that for a very long time. It has preached the love of

God at the price of its own humanity and has therefore ignored the implications of the Incarnation. Yet no 'new theology' is needed to make the point. The story of the Good Samaritan makes it better than any learned treatise. The parable of the Last Judgment makes it with shattering clarity. These narratives are not about religion. They are about life—with or without love.

There is, then, in this age as in every age, a spiritual choice between commitment to men and withdrawal from men; between humanity and inhumanity. And *this* humanity is divine. There is no need to go to the new theologians for the rehabilitation of man. It was all done in the Incarnation. God, by sharing our humanity, raised us to the status of his divinity. The early Greek Fathers (as opposed to most of the Latin) made much of this. The Orthodox Church still does. Yet it, like the others, has developed religious ways of by-passing the implications.

The 'new theology' is truly radical, a true expression of the roots of faith, when it turns men into men for others. The 'old theology' is equally radical when it does this. Men like Trevor Huddleston and Martin Luther King are, on the whole, products of the 'old'. The younger radicals in many parts of the world are largely products of the 'new'. But the distinction is wholly false. They are all simply people who are prepared to love and to pay a price. They need not even be Christians. Love suffices. 'Who was neighbour to him . . . ?' is an ethical, not a religious question. Salvation by works? Let me take refuge in Bonhoeffer, better rooted than I in the classics of the Reformation. He was in no doubt that the idea of cheap grace has been the downfall of many more Christians than any call to good works. Faith *means* works, or it is dead. Mere belief in God, even in his power to save, is of little consequence. If there is a devil, *he* certainly believes in God!

One of the troubles with the Church is that it continues to condemn Pelagius. It enshrines human irresponsibility. Pelagius was surely more right than his detractors in affirming man's ability, thanks to God's creativity, to choose to do what is right. 'We contradict the Lord to his face when we say "... we cannot, we are men; we are encompassed with fragile flesh". ... O unholy audacity! We charge the God of all knowledge with a two-fold ignorance, that he does not seem to know what he has made nor what he has commanded, as though, forgetting the human weakness of which he himself is the author, he imposed laws upon man which he cannot obey.'

The preoccupation of so much western theology with sin—and maybe St Paul *is* partly to blame—has obscured the possibility of man living in co-operation with God. The fall is taken much more seriously than the atonement. Sin is declared to be invincible this side of the grave. The result: a religion divorced from life, because life is inevitably corrupt. Consequently the extraordinary idea prevails that a 'religious', a man or woman divorced from the world, is nearer God than a secular man. This is religion indeed, primitive religion! Not the faith of the New Testament! Protestant and catholic variants of this escapist pietism are identical, however much their rationale may appear to differ. In each case salvation lies in religion, not in life. Yet not only does this conflict sharply with the nature of Christ, it flies in the face of all that the social prophets of the Old Testament preached. There faith was one of total political involvement to the point of vicarious suffering. Much of the Church has reverted to a religion more pagan than anything known to the people of Israel who, however disobedient, knew that justice was their business.

There *is* also a long Christian tradition of involvement for the world in conflict with a recurrent Constantinian sell-out to the world; like that of the priest who officiates at the commissioning of a nuclear bomber. William Blake was giving proper expression to the Gospel tradition when (in *Jerusalem*) he asked: 'Are not religion and politics the same thing? Brotherhood is religion.' If *that* is religion, then religionless Christianity is nonsense. This is a restoration of the word to its right and proper use. Restoration of religion is more constructive than abolition—the issue is not merely linguistic. There is a strangely sound Anglo-Saxon instinct that religion is about doing good. The churches have never managed to kill it. Religion is, of course, in its properly restored sense, about *being* good, but there is no legitimate distinction between being and doing. That, surely, is what Jesus is all about—only to a unique degree. His love for us remains, regardless of our ethical response.

Blake links politics with brotherhood—and both with

religion. The secular theologians are once again doing just that. It is what Harvey Cox is doing in *The Secular City*. The subject is man. The search is for true humanism; to enable man to be himself, to build the sort of society in which it will be more possible. It is to end man's alienation from himself, in ghettos of his own devising. And it is to do battle with man's inhumanity to man.

Is this *new* theology? No one who knows the scriptures would make any such claim. Nor should anyone rashly agree that St Paul did not understand—not, at any rate, if he is author of the First Letter to the Corinthians! Or to the Romans!—'Love is the fulfilling of the law.' Isaiah knew it all too; knew, too, what religion was *not* about: 'Is this the fast that I have chosen? Is it for a man ... to bow down his head as a bulrush and to spread sackcloth and ashes under him? ... Is not *this* the fast: to loose the bands of wickedness, to undo the heavy burdens and to let the oppressed go free, and to break every yoke? Is it not to share your bread with the hungry and to share your house with the homeless poor?'

This is contemporary, and it is political. It is the substance of religion, if the word is to be restored to its proper dignity. If religion is cultic escape it is both inhuman and unchristian. If religion is social commitment it is essential both to humanity and to christianity. There is no conflict between humanism and a religion which sees 'that of God' in every man. The terrifying parable of the last judgment goes further. It invalidates any ethical distinction between God and our neighbour.

None of this is properly called 'new theology'. And yet the Church has now for so long predominantly presented a picture of neo-pagan religiosity that it all *seems* to be new. The restoration of the Gospel to its social (and therefore political) reality is not made easier by a recent and brief period of religious history—between the First and Second World Wars—when a facile 'social Gospel' appeared to sweep the Church, with its assumptions about rapid progress to universal peace and justice, totally ignoring the realities of our personal and corporate depravity. The gas chambers of Auschwitz killed all that stone dead. Hitler served the devil better than he knew. With the horrors of World War II and the nuclear era which it inaugurated, theology retreated into its religious ghetto. The theology of the Kingdom was buried.

In consequence, the Marxist interpretation of religion seemed once again to be justified. Its real function seemed to be to provide a metaphysical apologia for the status quo. The Church had once again despaired of changing the world, the only thing which, from a properly human point of view, justifies its existence.

Where to lay the blame? There are many possibilities. To begin with, there was the reactionary, power-centred, wealth and privilege-protecting Vatican, casting a long shadow of pseudo-faith around the world. Afraid of revolution, allied to fascism in its pathological fear of communism, an apparently monolithic structure, it was worldly in almost every sense where divine-human prophecy was needed, and remotely religious where the world cried out to be loved and understood. In protestantism the problems were more complex. The reactions were no better. Reinhold Niebuhr, the voice of the disillusioned between the wars, came to stand for the abandonment of the vision of the New Jerusalem. At best, it was thought that Christians could influence secular structures sufficiently to turn great evils into lesser ones.

Where does that leave Christ, telling us that we are called to do greater works than he? Called, and therefore presumably able.

The answer is no easy one. But it must be a social one. Hans Jürgen Schultz points to it in this little book. It is the answer striven for by the many who feel that they must break out of traditional structures in order to discover what the world is about. These are not the people asking religious questions about whether or not God is dead, playing abstruse conceptual games and providing new and 'with it' escape mechanisms. They are the people who waste no time with arguments about the unknowable. They are as diverse as John XXIII and Danilo Dolci, Mario Borelli and Albert H. van den Heuvel, Bishop Skelton of Bulawayo and Professor Hromadka of Prague, Martin Niemöller and Trevor Huddleston, Pasternak and Martin Luther King. They are representative human beings who are determined that humanity shall triumph. They are secular saints, some openly Christian and some not at all. There is room in their company for atheists and communists. There is room for all who are concerned in concrete ways with making the world fit for divine beings to live in. And—does it need to be repeated?—by that I mean *human* beings.

Where is this battle for humanity being fought? Where war is declared efficiently on poverty and hunger, where freedom and truth are pursued relentlessly, where the world's prisoners are set free. Where money is used not to accrue wealth for the rich but to share the world's goods with the poor. Where men pursue peace by insisting on justice and by practising forgiveness. Where the family of man takes precedence over national, racial and religious interests. Where the answer to the question: would you like *your* daughter to marry a black man? is 'Yes—provided she loves *him*, and not just the idea.' The battle for humanity is won where the needs of men triumph over the demands of ideology, where truth penetrates the social filters which shelter us from reality and brain-wash us by techniques too subtle even for the brainwashers to recognize.

The battle is being fought where the structures of the Church and of the world are geared to creative change. In the offices of Christian Aid where, at a British level, and under the competent direction of one woman of vision, Janet Lacey, administration works well to feed some of the world's hungry, administration that is now being geared to persuading the nation that this task can ultimately only be done by radical political change in Britain and all the other wealthy nations.

The same battle for humanity is being fought in the offices of Christian Action where, largely through the vision of one man, Canon John Collins, the Defence and Aid Fund is administered to help the victims of South Africa's (and now Rhodesia's) *apartheid* laws. Through the Fund men and women are able to receive at least such justice as money can buy—and when they are put behind bars their families are not left totally destitute.

The battle is being fought in the offices of Amnesty International where again, initially through the vision of one man, Peter Benenson, work goes on to set men and women free in almost every country of the world— people who, for no humanly adequate reason, are in prison. The world's prisoners of conscience.

Perhaps these cases are obvious. They are still far from obvious to most churchgoers. The maxim 'do not mix religion and politics' still holds among most would-be Christians. And what they mean is: do not let the Church get caught up with changing the world. There's no knowing where that might lead to. True, there isn't. There is no security in taking up the cause of man. It may lead to a cross. Jesus assured his disciples that it would. 'And that won't do the Church any good.' No, in fact it will almost certainly put an end to the Church as we know it. St Paul's insight that it is in 'dying that we live' is utterly relevant. For that reason obedient Christians are virtually bound to be subversive churchmen.

What St Paul calls the warfare of the spirit is a tremendous challenge which the Church, as now constituted, is simply not equipped to fight. At best there are at the moment a few auxiliary regiments equipped with the right weapons. The main body of the army is obsoletely equipped and quite untrained. At this point it becomes clear that the obviously effective fighters (like those mentioned above) merely serve to provide the rest of us with an alibi. The answers or the weapons are only to be found in the world itself, in secular society. The sociologists and the technologists are today in the vanguard of the battle for humanity. At least the possibility of being truly human is within their grasp. So is the possibility of being totally inhuman. Almost limitless creativity opens up undreamed of possibilities for *all* men. Now we really *can* do much greater things than Jesus in healing, feeding, *fulfilling*. We can equally well totally destroy. We can begin anew to create brotherhood in God's 'holy mountain'. Or we can destroy it and all living things on it.

We are free, as never before, to choose between life and death. The implication of being converted to the world is a readiness to shoulder this total responsibility. That is the significance of man's much spoken of 'coming of age'. We are not only free to choose, but free to implement our choices. We are free to live, or to die— together.

And that demands a newly worked out social theology. Happily it is already in the process of development, and the intellectual stimuli come from the far corners of the earth. Latin Americans, Africans and Asians possibly have more important things to say than Europeans. Secularization is far bigger than merely slotting the Church into the structures of the technocratic society. If that were all it was, it might well be no more than a 'no change' signal. The Church, snugly cuddled into its niche of modern society, is precisely what the Gospel forbids. In that sense, in the sense that secularization merely means adaptation (in order to ensure relatively undisturbed survival), it is a real menace. It is conservative and not progressive.

The Vatican Council clearly revealed this split. Leaving aside the minority of head-in-the-sand reactionaries, the 'progressive' bishops were divided into radicals and conservatives, divided between those who were prepared to see the Church as it is die, in order to give it new and vital life, and those who wanted to up-date the Church merely to prevent it from dying. No one seriously doubts that the latter group was the larger. An important question is: to which group does Pope Paul belong? All the indications are that he himself does not know the answer and is struggling to find it. That answer may be vital. It will certainly help to determine the future of structures and institutions which, as they are, impede the Gospel and therefore stand in the way of humanity.

Charles Davis, in leaving the Church of Rome, saw this clearly. In his *Observer* apologia he wrote: 'I should take more kindly to (the Church's) constant anxiety over the institution, were it not true that the Church in recent history has again and again compromised its mission to save its institutional existence or privilege. The glaring instance is the Church in Nazi Germany, but this does not stand alone. When, in fact, has the Church ever entered into conflict with established authority to bear witness, even at the cost of its institutional position? The Church as an institution is turned in upon itself and more concerned with its own authority and prestige than with the Gospel message. I cannot accept its claim upon my faith.'

Davis' indictment does not stop there. The Church is accused of being unconcerned with truth and uncaring about people. He is surely right in his analysis, however much his *apparent* opting out may be open to legitimate debate.

Some have questioned Davis' statement about the Church in Nazi Germany, having in mind the many martyrs, catholic and protestant. The answer is sad but inescapable. The martyrs trod their lonely path despite the institutions of the Church, not because of them. The story of one man suffices to stand for all. Jaegerstätter was a faithful catholic peasant who refused to fight in Hitler's unjust wars. His Bishop told him he was in error. He died without the Church's blessing for his obedience to Christ. There were very few like him. And even retrospectively the official Church refuses to 're-habilitate' him.

German protestantism, through the famous Stuttgart 'Declaration of Guilt', did try to make formal amends, but it has ever since been on the brink of surrender to institutional reaction. Davis' critique is applicable in full to all our churches, in particular his recognition that Christians show no passionate concern for truth. Truth cannot be enshrined in credal statements. It is alive. It is the world *as it is*, confronted with a living immanent and transcendent God. Truth is a recognition of reality, just as freedom is a recognition of necessity. The only reality we know is the world of our neighbour. The only necessity we know is the need to love—and be loved. Can the Church face *this* conversion?

Not only the Church needs converting. All the world's ideologists and idealists are in much the same position— not to speak of the hopeless nihilists and the not alto- gether unattractive escapists into one form or another of the 'playboy philosophy'. There is not all that much time for this conversion to take effect. I do not pretend to understand the dynamics of history but it suffices to read my daily newspaper to be left in little doubt that if things in the world do not soon begin to improve, they will get a lot worse. Other men see this too—and some of them are Christian. They then begin to find it almost impossible to operate within the structures of the Church. This need happily not worry them too much, for those caught up in the web of ecclesiastical struc- tures are a minority, mostly clergy. But this in its turn should not obscure the fact that increasingly over the last few years the 'religious' top people have been far ahead of their followers in the degree of their commit- ment to the world.

This commitment exploded in an exciting way in the

midst of the Vatican Council. It was communicated with apostolic authenticity by a number of bishops: by one for example who, in the face of the poverty of his people in Brazil, had abdicated his own position of privilege and wealth and had become a servant of the poorest—identified with them. This same spirit broke out in an equally elemental way at the World Council of Churches' conference on Church and Society in 1966. Here, white men were in a minority. The revolutionary voice of a hungry, oppressed world, seemed for a moment to be, at the same time and perhaps for the first time, a Christian voice.

At quite another level the conversion is moving apace. In a process of ideological 'revisionism' common to them both, Marxists and Christians have begun to discover each other. The widespread Christian-Marxist dialogue is no more than a symptom of the triumph of humanity over ideas which, isolated from experienced truth, are not only dead but deadly. The Christian-Marxist attempt at a common understanding of *what men need* is also a recognition of one another's humanity —and of one another's 'saints'. If communists today are quick to quote Pope John as 'their man' (true, in the only sense that matters: he loved them), so Christians should hasten to see 'their man' in a communist such as Abram Fischer, the South African lawyer whose court testimony against *apartheid*, prior to his life sentence, is one of the most moving of all human documents.

There is only one humanity. Man's destiny is to join it—or perish. Yet this must be no high flown emotional commitment to principles or even to men. It must increasingly be the application of love through what appear to be impersonal processes. Commitment to a world crying for peace and bread must be a commitment to a mastery of the social processes of radical change. Slogans will not do it. Neither will sentiments. What is needed is a hard-headed application of economics, social theory and technological capacity. Hard headed, but warm hearted. Commitment to humanism is a prerequisite. At that point the hard work begins.

The task is for all. The Christian is privileged only in the sense that he already knows that success is possible—and indeed assured. As for the Church, whatever it looks like tomorrow, it will need to gear in to the world as it is, without selling out to it. It will need to redeploy its resources of men and wealth as radically as any obsolete industry. It will need to ask searching questions, expecting answers. It will need to learn simple lessons such as the one that men in society need a new vision of their role as human beings in a cybernetic age: they need technical and human vision, not thousands of obsolete religious buildings (costing millions) and some 30,000 parsons of one brand or another in England alone.

Conversion to the world means that the people of God (all people, potentially) should be equipped to change society, instead of standing on the sidelines to criticize. It means a Church politically committed, economically vulnerable, humanly efficient and at the same time open to attack by the world. It means a return to the Hebrew and Christian tradition which allows of no distinction between the sacred and the secular. It means action; 'Christian' action only because it is genuinely human. It means putting an end once and for all to the degrading concept that something is 'merely' human. Auschwitz, Dresden, Hiroshima and Vietnam today are not manifestations of 'mere' humanity. They only illustrate our freedom to choose inhumanity, to embrace death rather than life. Heaven and Hell are here and now; to choose between. The Church will only be the Church if it makes its choice—not vaguely and on general principles, but day by day, politically and dangerously, for, to quote Blake's *Jerusalem* again: 'He who would do good to another, must do it in minute particulars. General good is the plea of the scoundrel, hypocrite and flatterer.'

The plea of Schultz's book is not a new one. But its language and style are new, and particularly new in the German context. The author relies on no 'school' of theology. His plea for a frankly political style of discipleship is bound to shock. It is very much part of the breath of fresh air blowing through the churches. There can be no doubt at all; Schultz is part of the Church. He has not opted out. And he is in harmony with what is probably the most creative of German protestant thought, Jürgen Moltmann's *Theology of Hope*[1], which faces up to the political implications of eschatology and finds common ground with parts of modern revisionist Marxism. Harvey Cox, very much of a counterpart to Schultz in the American scene, writes of the author and

[1] SCM Press, 1967.

his friends: 'They could in some measure be grouped as "worldly thinkers", as opposed to the others who, regardless of their alleged radical position, still busy themselves with "religious" questions. There is a parallel in nineteenth-century philosophy. Karl Marx, though an avid atheist in his early years, soon tired of arguing about God and decided that the question would only be settled when the social deformation giving rise to the idea of God was corrected. Other philosophers had talked about the world, he said, but now the time had come to change it. *Conversion to the World* is not a Marxist book, but it does breathe some of its same conviction. The theological questions which pester us today will not be settled by talking about them some more. New insights will arise from action. The Church will be granted a message for the world only when it takes that world with unconditional seriousness.'

It is my conviction that conversion to this world *may* spring from a personal experience of the compassion of Christ. Equally well, that conversion may have to precede a rediscovery of the God whom some have (not for the first time) put in a tomb.

And none of this is new. It has all been said in the Bible, and better said. It has all been analysed by the much neglected early Fathers. A minority of Christians (and Jews!) have never allowed it to be forgotten. Humanists of the enlightenment have carried the flame when it was in danger of extinction. Apostles of East and West have lived the social Gospel. The Christian socialists of the nineteenth and twentieth century from

Maurice and Kingsley to Temple and Bell have not shied away from involvement with political realities. Prophets like Conrad Noel, St John Groser and Stanley Evans, 'High Church' Anglicans all three, have not been afraid to face rejection while, in their parishes and up and down the land, they preached that the *Magnificat* had more in common with the 'Red Flag' than with 'Rule Britannia' ... and that property, in times of unemployment and hunger, *is theft*. And George MacLeod and Donald Soper are still with us, Lords maybe, but as they would hasten to add, no more lords of God's creation than every one of us, if only we chose to take our seat.

Secularization is neither good nor bad. It all depends what we make of it. Nicholas Berdyaev, using yesterday's language, speaks prophetically about tomorrow's world. To quote him at some length is as good an introduction to Hans Jürgen Schultz as I can think of:

'The problem of man takes precedence over that of society or of culture, and here man is to be considered, not in his inner spiritual life, not as an abstract spiritual being, but as an integral being, social and cosmic ... Only a form of Socialism, which unites personality and the communal principle, can satisfy Christianity. The hour has struck when, after terrible struggle, after an unprecedented de-Christianization of the world ... Christianity will be revealed in its true form ... what it stands for and stands against ... It will be seen to stand for man and for humanity, for the value of dignity of personality, for freedom, for social justice, for the brotherhood of men and of nations, for enlightenment, for the creation of new life.

'(In the past) Christians have often left social reforms in the hands of others, they have often even done injustice and consented to adapting higher spiritual values in the interests of the ruling class and the established order. They have succeeded in producing a bourgeois Christianity. And now the most merciless judgment is being passed upon it . . .

'Christian piety all too often has seemed to be the withdrawal from the world and from men, a sort of transcendent egoism, the unwillingness to share the suffering of the world and man . . . It lacked human warmth. And the world has risen in protest against this form of piety . . . Against this protest, only a reborn piety can stand. Care for the life of another . . . *Bread for myself is a material question: bread for my neighbour is a spiritual question.*

'(This new piety) cannot permit human slavery to cosmic or social and technical forces. It calls man to a kingly role, and to creative work in the world. The new Christian . . . does not curse the world, neither does he condemn the possessed and the idolatrous. He shares the suffering of the world, bears in his body the tragedy of man.

'In the old forms of Christian piety love of God meant lack of love for man . . . The only possible escape from this is in a new piety in which the love of God will be love for man as well, and where freedom from the powers of this world will at the same time mean love for all God's creation, a religion in which man's spiritual life will be . . . creative in the world, as well.

'Christianity is above all else a religion of love and liberty, but just because of this, the future is not determined by blind fate, either for good or for evil. Hence we move forward toward a tragic conflict. The new Christianity must rehumanize man and society, culture and the world. But for Christianity this process of humanization is something not merely human; it is Divine-human, of the nature of the God-man. Only in Divine-humanity, in the Body of Christ, can man be saved. Otherwise he will be torn to pieces by demonic forces, by the demons of hatred and malice.'[1]

Nicholas Berdyaev's language is not mine, nor is it Schultz's. A humiliated and defenceless Church must go out into a hostile world to re-discover the God-man in the least of his brethren. The new piety is that conversion to the world which Berdyaev had experienced, to which Hans Jürgen Schultz points and which we must expect more surely on the Underground to Piccadilly than on a pilgrimage to the 'Holy Land'. More than likely, however well forewarned, we shall fail to recognize the neighbour on *our* road to Emmaus. May he open our eyes.

[1] Nicholas Berdyaev, *The Fate of Man in the Modern World*, SCM Press, 1935.

I

A WORLD WITHOUT RELIGION

What is dangerous about our situation today is that our present intellectual equipment is inadequate to cope with a technological world. The metaphysics that has served us hitherto, whether materialistic, idealistic or Christian, is incapable of closing the gap between us and the fateful advent of this era of technology . . .

MARTIN HEIDEGGER

This Unmastered Age

MARXISM has all but abandoned its polemical and anti-Christian campaign 'to substantiate the truth of the here-and-now'. Roles have been strangely reversed. For atheism now seems to be taken more seriously and to be better appreciated by Christians than by those who claim to be its proponents. Compared with the radical conclusions of Dietrich Bonhoeffer, today's professional atheists in East and West have been able to offer mere crumbs, overlaid with inconsequential icing. Bonhoeffer not only accepted verbatim some of Marx's and Feuerbach's direct attacks on transcendental religion, he systematically and radically drove these attacks home. 'Atheists bore me,' says Schnier in Heinrich Böll's novel *Ansichten Eines Clowns*, 'they are always talking about God.'

The real debate on atheism, its truth and its error, has yet to take place. Atheism is commonly practised, but its true significance is far from being understood. We are stubbornly wedded to a traditional attitude that is assumed to be in opposition to atheism. Our religion is both defended and attacked on that assumption. There is in our scheme of things a material and a spiritual realm, a profane and a sacred, a realm of fact and a realm of faith, a realm of this world and a realm of the world to come. Our way of thinking is still shot through with the Greek habit of splitting reality, with a dualism between God and world, body and soul, heaven and earth, up above and down below. Almost unconsciously we have fallen victim to a crypto-Platonism. Our denials notwithstanding, we cling to a metaphysical currency that has ceased to be valid.

What was once automatically designated as spiritual is now generally open to a rational explanation. We no longer need to fall back on 'working hypotheses'. The formerly normative belief in a realm that is not of this world is rooted in conditions and assumptions that belong to a past age. Explanations in secular terms are now to hand. In fact yesterday's 'other-worldliness' has a perfectly sound explanation, which can now be given in terms of the here-and-now. It expressed the fears and hopes of men in terms that may no longer make sense

34

to us but which, in their day, made very good sense.
Yesterday truth was encountered in symbols which
were an honest and useful basis for thought and action.
Today these symbols have become a burden to us. They
were once integrating influences; today they have the
effect of imposing a false dualism on us. What past
generations took as much for granted as their mother
tongue has now been reduced to mere metaphor, highly
problematical and certainly affording no basis for
action. It is not that we are honest, whereas previous
generations were not, or that they were steeped in faith,
while we are reduced to superficial rationalism. It is
simply that we live in a different sort of world.

This is not the place to delve deeply into the nature
of our new condition. Nor is there opportunity to
unravel the complexities of such elusive phenomena.
Were I to try, I should almost certainly fail. I shall
therefore merely attempt to describe our condition in
barest outline.

We are today at the end of two great epochs of human
history. As early as 1913 Charles Péguy wrote that 'the
world has seen greater changes in the last thirty years
than in the two thousand that preceded them'. Practi-
cally all the many attempts to describe our condition
are therefore bound to prove inadequate. None of the
names given to our age wholly describe it. Generally
they are relevant to some aspect of it that is already out
of date. It will not do to speak of 'the end of the modern
era'. Our era is itself, as is becoming ever more obvious,
merely the end of an historical process that spans

several millennia. The new age is the beginning of an end which can no longer be hidden. It is not surprising then that Brecht devotes one of his dramas to Galileo. He puts into the mouth of the physicist a comment which is meant as a comment on *our* times: 'Today is the 6th January 1610. Man enters in his diary: There is no more heaven.' Physics are in; metaphysics out.

Whereas once within the ordered firmament of undisturbed celestial motion, man took for granted or even measured the reflection of divine being, now we are suddenly confronted with the unfathomable infinity of silent spaces. The concept of heaven above and hell beneath has become untenable. Earth is just one planet circling its sun. In the atom the physicist observes processes which compare with the movement of the planets. The universe no longer has a fixed upper and lower region. The old images are defective and along with them the terms, structures and ideas with which we used to describe truths about man and his world. We still go back to these old notions for comfort. We are afraid to admit that the earth is no longer central but peripheral. We no longer see it as a fixed point at the heart of things. It is on the circumference. In the cosmic interplay it is only one factor among many. Knowledge of this changes every relationship. It is enough to make us lose our bearings. Our consciousness of self is subjected to a revolution the effect of which we cannot even predict—and all this three hundred and fifty years after Galileo.

The fundamental process that must occupy us if we

want to understand and define our age is the secularization of the whole of life. No area—most certainly not the Church—is beyond the scope of this process. People may condemn it, conduct campaigns to oppose it, and yet it is part of the very air that we breathe. Secularization is comprehensive and not merely a partial phenomenon of the modern world. It is not a theory or plan that can be put alongside other theories and plans. It is a fact from which we cannot escape by persistently ignoring it.

True, we can explain the world as though it were not a secularized world. But then the explanation would not tally with our own experience. It would be an alien and incongruous explanation. It would stand in isolation, independent of experience, whereas the two should interpenetrate and be a corrective to each other. The discrepancy between our actual experience of the world and of the traditional interpretation of its nature is our real dilemma. The present time remains to a considerable extent unexplained, inarticulate. We do not know by what name to call it. We have yet to come to terms with it.

Rapid change is most evident in the field of the natural sciences and of technology. We can now put to use the most profound insights into the physical order. Hitherto all improvements in life have depended on natural sources of energy, mainly coal and oil. We have learnt to turn these into the warmth, electricity and light which are indispensable to us and which in turn are used to provide clothing and food, transport and the means of communication. With the exhaustion of the world's coal and oil, the world's economy, as we know it, would collapse. But now atomic energy is beginning to take their place. Its release is the most significant achievement of science and technology. Our future depends on it. This is true in a positive and in a negative sense. Its immense potential for good is balanced by its deadly possibilities. They go hand in hand. The same means which can ensure the future of mankind can also destroy it. And it is to this very destructiveness that men are devoting themselves, putting much greater effort into preparing for the wrong uses of atomic energy than into working for the extension of human existence.

We have acquired knowledge and know-how without possessing a commensurate standard of human conduct. There is a fatal discrepancy between the means we have devised to give expression to a responsible society and both the extent of our knowledge and the power to use it. We do not know by what criteria to judge our own actions. We live in a scientific and technological age. Yet we lack an awareness of its significance and an ethic relevant to it. We desperately lack motives, guidelines, criteria and categories of thought which measure up to our situation and which will help us to master it.

Speaking of the problem of war, Carl Friedrich von Weizsäcker reduces the alternatives to this formula: 'The nuclear age forces us to abolish war. Failing that, war will abolish us.' Peace has become a prerequisite for the modern world. This peace should not, as von

Weizsäcker says, be equated with the 'golden age'. 'The issue is not the elimination of conflicts but the elimination of a particular way of resolving conflicts. This is an inevitable consequence of modern technology.' War is based on an illusory presupposition. To contemplate it is no way of getting to grips with a problem; rather it is a refusal to face up to it. Rather than master a problem, war is an attempt to eliminate the problem. There is an inner logic about our age which inevitably faces the peoples of the world with the need to abandon their illusions. They will need to settle for peace. Peace, of course, is something more than the absence of war. For that reason the mere prevention of the explosion of the nuclear bomb is, in the long run, insufficient. What is needed is a total and unparalleled reappraisal, calling for a degree of maturity and endeavour for which we are ill prepared. What we have yet to learn in this era of technology is to act in a manner compatible with its demands.

The threats posed by our inability to take responsible actions which fit the tools at our disposal, are not confined to international politics, although it is in this field that these threats are most obvious. They have long since become the most mundane of problems; problems of man's humanity in a world which we constantly manipulate and yet fail to control.

What I am trying to say is well illustrated by Max Frisch in his *Diary*, in the course of an observation about himself. He is sitting in an aircraft. Flying over a small town that looks like an architect's model he realizes, without wanting to, that he would be quite capable of bombing this peaceful plot of earth. 'No need for any patriotic fury or even a prolonged campaign of hatred,' he observes. 'All that is needed is a railway station, a factory with numerous chimneys, a steamer at the jetty and I'm dying to put in a stick of bombs. And in no time it's all over. I watch the steamer rolling over. The street is like an ant-hill when you push a twig into it. And maybe I'd see the chimneys buckling at the knees and crashing in a cloud of dust. I see no blood, I hear no one dying. Everything is clean, at an inhuman distance, almost amusing. Not without danger to myself either. I'm not pretending that it's harmless ... What gets me is the difference between dropping bombs on a model target far below that is at once a little charming, a little boring and certainly a little insignificant, and *being down there myself*, drawing my sheath knife and approaching a human being to kill him, one single human being whose face I shall see; maybe a man spreading manure or a woman knitting; maybe a child standing bare foot in a pond, crying because its paper ship is sinking. The latter is something I can't see myself doing. As for the former—and this is the crucial difference—I'm not so sure ... Were it not for our being divorced from the need to experience relationship, a divorce made possible in a multiplicity of ways by technology, it would probably be impossible to set up such large military establishments, obedient and ready for action at a moment's notice. And I'm not implying that people would be any better than they are now.

Not all of us would make good butchers, but nearly all of us are fit to be soldiers, standing behind the big guns, looking at our watches and pulling the cord. Strange, how distances that can be measured in yards should make so much difference; that our imagination is so weak . . .'

Max Frisch has only chosen one small example. It would not be difficult to adduce much more serious symptoms which show how far the world has left us behind. We must learn to make ourselves at home in this new world. Technology has severed our direct relationship both with people and with things. In face of this loss of immediacy and of the ever-increasing complexity of all relationships any naïve approach to the world is bound to be inadequate. Categories like instinct, or conscience, or mere good-will will simply not cope with the situation. They can no longer be relied upon. Both in small things and in great we need to acquire self-awareness that is related to the real world. We need to evaluate and direct our own capabilities and to reflect on them purposefully. We must confront technology with infinitely more open and astute minds than in the past. An attitude that measures up to the challenge of technology can only be acquired as we become aware of the far-reaching implications of that challenge.

The Enlightenment of Faith

In this unaccustomed situation faith is called upon to give an account of itself, to reveal its nature. Will it dispense us from the *duty to think*? Will it remain in conflict with the reason and intellectual integrity which a technical world demands? Or will faith help to ensure that the scientific basis of life in the world does not itself transgress against reason and humanity? The plenipotentiary nature of man (Gen. 1.28) today has global significance. But mankind's function has in fact always been a universal one. Once this was mere theory; today it is necessity. Our faith and man's service to the whole world are closely interrelated, yet the nature of this relationship is still largely undiscovered. Faith should stimulate, enlighten and encourage man in his attempt to serve the world. It should be both the impulse of and the corrective to a reasoned and planned attempt to master the inescapable problems posed by the world. *Faith is not the opposite of reason but the assurance of its truth.* It is the guarantor of knowledge.

The criteria of faith may be thought to have changed. That is not only true in a European context. It is true everywhere, not least in Asia where faith is no longer a matter of comparative (or competitive) religion but is considered in terms of its relevance to the modern world. Asia is in the midst of a religious revival or renaissance. But this much-spoken-of return to religion should not deceive us into ignoring the nascent secularization which is breaking through the ancient culture and religiosity of a land like India, breaking through as the sun breaks through the morning mist. In Asia as elsewhere the intellectuals tend to equate religion with superstition. The Marxists see it as an opiate. Nehru described factory chimneys as the temples of modern India. 'Ultimately only this world and this life are of interest to me,' he writes, 'not some other world or some future life. I do not know whether there is a life after death, and, important as these questions may be, I must confess that they in no way concern me.'

Whatever one's view of the current concept of the *end of religion*, there is no getting away from the fact that the function and significance of religion is subject to inevitable and rapid change dictated by the new nature of our relationship with the world, a relationship transformed by technological influences. In India it was once possible to say: *everything* here is religion. But technology brings a degree of enlightenment and of this-worldliness with it that cannot be withstood. And this brings in train a totally changed mentality. The well-known words of Ibn Saud crop up everywhere, in one form or another: 'I have imported machines from Europe, but I will have none of Europe's irreligion!' This reveals an utterly inadequate appreciation of the nature and significance of what is known as secularization. Technology is more than the sum total of machinery. Technology is the product of attitude which does not think in religious but in historical terms. Its intellectual framework is based on historicity. It gives rise to a standard of human conduct which cannot be adduced from traditional concepts in the realm of religion.

The world has begun to function without religious presuppositions and to function just as well as it did before. It has been said that artificial fertilizer has

replaced real manure. A flash of lightning no longer
sends us scurrying into monastic cloisters. We are not
concerned with how to escape the world. We are more
interested in bending it to our will and rationally
ordering its affairs. We are less concerned with the
world's origin than with its future. Instead of delving
into the past we are taking responsibility for tomorrow's
world. Cultic religion is being superseded by a secular
'diaconate', by service to the world. We are reticent to
speak of God, of Christ, of eternity. No longer do these
words trip lightly off our tongue. We impose a certain
verbal chastity on ourselves in these matters. But when
it comes to the meaning of life, of humanity, when it
comes to the nature of hope, our senses have come alive.
That is not to say that God, Christ and eternity were
merely convenient symbols for life, humanity and hope.
Yet when there is talk of the one set of concepts the
other is inevitably involved. If that is not the case then
neither is *really* being discussed. To turn to life, to
humanity, to hope, must inevitably encompass a return
to God, to Christ, to eternity.

Symptoms such as these point to a structural change
in man which is of immense significance. Religion in
this context turns out to be an embarrassment, a sign of
dishonesty, an alibi for those who either cannot cope
with the world or who despise it. This 'religion' will not
concede that the once relevant questions centred on
human existence have now become centred on human
conduct. The significance of the world is no longer of
interest; its discernible nature is. What we impute to

the world ceases to matter. But we are desperately eager to discover what the world has in store for us. To this we seek an answer with unparalleled intensity. We do not want to see the world transfigured. We do want to see it explained. The substance of things is of no concern; their function on the other hand enthrals us. Our attitude to nature is no longer contemplative but pragmatic. The natural sciences are made to serve technology. Human insight is made to serve production. Man who was once constantly confronted with what was new and strange now comes face to face almost exclusively with concepts to which he himself has given birth. We must even accept the idea that man himself is the product of planning and that a specific type of man is subject to manipulation.

The world lacks an essential signpost to something beyond itself. It is true, largely as a result of the insights of natural science but also on the strength of the ever present evidence of man's limitations, that we are becoming more modest and less demanding than many previous generations. We are no longer naïve enough to think we can wholly grasp the meaning of the universe. Since man has learnt that the world is round he can no longer see all of it from one vantage point. And so we are more interested in opinions than in systems of thought. A sketch plan is of greater interest to us than an all-embracing blue-print. We speak of the openness of the world, of its incompleteness and of our inability to 'take it over'. We meet the world in history. We experience it in terms of encounter and of relationship. Any description we give to it can have only relative validity. There *can* be no ultimate judgment. What is possible and likely has greater reality than what is calculable and therefore calls for no degree of trust on our part.

And yet for us this one world which we must seek to fathom cannot be seen through at a glance. We are confronted with a world which we must order. We must discover its secrets, unravel its problems; none of which can be done by falling back on a discernible authority external to the world, in terms of which everything else becomes meaningful. This cannot be done unless peripheral issues are brought to the centre and made normative, unless the insignificant becomes the happy hunting ground of the theologians who content themselves with making God relevant to the gaps in human understanding; unless we create a God good only for the emergencies with which we cannot cope. This will not do. The world must be made to reveal its own mysteries.

There is no denying that sorrow, death, insecurity and perplexity are here and here to stay. So are the hidden things of life and the unforeseen. But they provide no new evidence. They are integral parts of one reality. They are just as much part of secular experience as more concrete and obvious phenomena. Nothing gives them any particular affinity with any sphere beyond the world. They are certainly not a blank space on the map, under the jurisdiction of the Church. The gaps in our understanding cannot be adduced as proofs of the existence of God. Our need of God cannot be deduced from the state of the world as we know it, from its incompleteness, from its need of fulfilment. Integrity makes this road to God an impossible one to tread. Religion is no longer the context, or at any rate not the sole context, in which we meet God. Today this is something we may still be inclined to ignore. But what of 1984?

The world will no longer hear of the doctrine that man counts for nothing so that God may count for all. No longer are things seen in the light of the numinous, the divine, but rather in terms of what is human. This makes calls upon man which demand that he should 'come of age'. A certain adulthood is assumed which man cannot quite square with the present stage of his development. Too much is expected of man today. This characteristic of our era both gives rise to hope and is at the same time ominous. Man must prove himself. Only by his independence, responsibility and maturity can he realize his own nature, realize it as he copes with the dangers and problems of secularization.

The Discovery of the Greater Christ

It goes without saying that the secularization of the world implies the abandonment of important positions held by the Church. That is why Christians can hardly be said to have responded to this situation with enthusiasm. They face the present time as deeply estranged men, hurt, and aggressively on the defensive. They are aware of what they have lost, unaware of what they have gained. Their terms of reference are in the past, a

47

past that by and large confines itself to condemning the present state of the world. Christians are in the process of becoming the nightwatchmen of western civilization. They still seek to preserve what will and must go. They identify themselves with an era of cultural and social history within which they are comfortably at home; yet it is an epoch gone beyond recall. They pin their faith on assumptions which are no longer valid, invoke crises of no real importance and never really manage to bring themselves to face up to present realities.

The question whether this profoundly transforming crisis does not itself throw up a new and integrated way of life in which all things cohere and in the light of which men might look creatively and without embarrassment to the future—this question is either too vague or too self-confident. I am really asking with Friedrich Gogarten whether the impetus that has led to 'the end of metaphysics', to secularization and all that flows from it, has not all along been inherent in the Christian faith. I wonder whether something is not now working itself out which can only be explained in terms of church history, of the Incarnation of God, of his becoming 'world', of his entry into history, of his solidarity with our way of life, of his abolition of the dualism between the seen and the unseen, the sacred and the secular? Might there not be a decisive connection between Galileo's affirmation on January 6th, 1610 and the epiphany of God in the New Testament? It was Oswald Spengler who said that but for the medieval monk in his cell there could be no modern professor in his study or laboratory. But merely to state discernible historical causalities will not do. The real question today is—and this is once more of interest to the theologians—whether history A.D. is of a different quality from history B.C., a quality which now makes any attempt to exalt religion over secular history both irrelevant and confusing. The Incarnation both *concerns* the world and *changes it*; it is an historic event of universal and political significance, certainly not one concerned only with the ecclesiastical or the existential. That is why the commonly held view that only what can be personalized is theologically significant is untenable. Such a view fails to take into account the new reality that has entered the world in the incarnate Christ.

Protestant thought has been well protected against any variety of evolutionary perfectionism. In the process it has unwittingly fallen victim to the opposite tendency, to believe in a type of 'regressive evolution'. History has not been recognized as 'a great phenomenon of Christianization' (as Teilhard de Chardin saw it), but rather as a sad process of de-Christianization, as if each passing day constituted a greater divorce from New Testament origins and therefore an advance of evil in the face of the salvation that had come once and for all. But the problem of evolution apart—and anyway that is not our topic—we need to pose quite a different question at this point: is church history not in essence the unwritten history of its secular concomitants? Might it not be said that the most vigorous and impressive movements of our time are in fact boomerangs, once thrown by

Christians and long since forgotten? Carl Friedrich von Weizsäcker poses the question whether the miracles of modern technology do not correspond with the 'great works' which Christ said we would do, 'works greater than I'. Is the Church not latently present in innumerable situations? Does it not play a large part, however unverifiable, in many of the events and conflicts of our day? Is the Church not present where there is no church?

We are hesitant to define the boundaries of the Church. Traditional definitions no longer meet the case. We are faced with the phenomenon of an anonymous and unconscious everyday Christianity which makes nonsense of our ideas of a definable and institutionalized Church. The Church as we know it is too small to contain all that is properly embraced today by Christianity.

In our age of astronauts we are suddenly given new insights, shown new dimensions of the meaning of the Son of Man. Our breath is taken away. History will not stand still. We are driven inexorably to discover the 'greater Christ', the Ruler of All (*Pantokrator*), the Lord who overcomes the world with supra-personal power and who is in full control of the great openness of our age. This Christ has broken out of our church structures. He has fled from the churches. We must therefore find him in the anonymity in which he is at work among us. That is the nature of our discipleship. But we lack the inner drive for this new enterprise, we lack it because western Christendom is still tied to the tragic proposition

that *where the Church is, there is Christ also*. If only we
were to realize that the reverse is true: *where Christ is,
there the Church is also?* Surely he was always to be found
where he was least expected.

It is high time we accepted an idea that has always
been anathema to religious traditionalists, the idea that
salvation is also for the having outside the Church. If we
continue to exclude this possibility our concept of the
Church will not suffice to enable us to understand the
universal problems of the world, let alone to solve them.
The trouble is that our traditional, sterile, introspective
theology, which exhausts itself in wranglings of its own
making, is not disposed to ask such questions or to search
for answers. Theology has given itself the role of an
usherette, showing God to his place. Instead of observ-
ing where and how God acts, the theologians have
decided that they will *determine* it. Theology has been so
preoccupied with defining God's nature that it has been
blind to his action in the world. For centuries the
theologians have been so divorced from reality that
they are now incapable of commenting sensibly on
history as it unravels itself. That is why outsiders to the
Church, who are alert and eager to face the problems of
our time, can often reveal God's intention far better as
they observe him in the processes of natural science and
are prepared to take the risks of experimental observation. This is so, however little they may fit the traditional concepts of what a Christian is meant to be like.
The real questions of today are generally posed quite
untheologically by laymen.

Theology tends to confront reality with its own premises and to measure it by canonical yardsticks. As things are now this is not likely to alter. It means that reality, instead of being exposed by theology, is obscured by it. And so theology leads to its own impotence. If it is to recover its true purpose it will need to measure its dogmatic preconceptions against real experience, to reorientate them, to correct them, to risk losing them. It will need to reckon with the presence of God today. Theology at its best is concerned with giving contemporary reality to a Gospel which was committed to writing in a world of totally different assumptions and thought-patterns. Theology has the task of confronting this allegedly unchangeable Gospel with the world as it is and with interpreting the world in terms of that Gospel. But the Gospel is more than a historic document that calls for a modern translation; it is a contemporary event that will submit to no form of theological incarceration. The Gospel is the proclamation of news which, by its inherent nature, cannot be dated. Merely to project an interpretation of the Gospel into the world and to confront the world with it as though it were some law independent of history and existing outside it will not do either. The Gospel must be seen to speak out of the dynamic processes of history itself. We tend to regard Christians as purveyors of a cut and dried message. But they are also diviners searching for the basis and the 'happening' of the Gospel. This Gospel is not something they have passed by; it is still ahead of them. To be able to proclaim it means to be aware of and to discover the presence of Christ *incognito* in our world. The world is such an exciting place for Christians because this surprise encounter may take place at any moment.

2

THE ILLUSION OF A GODLESS WORLD

Industrial civilizations are by their nature atheist in character as agricultural civilizations were heathen. Faith in the true God is quite unaffected by this. As they become increasingly profane modern civilizations do face us with the danger of 'losing' God. Yet maybe they will give us the opportunity to discover him in greater depth. This discovery could pave the way for new syntheses while doing away, once and for all, with the effects of our primitive confusions.

HENRI DE LUBAC

The End of Metaphysics

WE find ourselves in a situation that is strangely paralleled by the beginnings of Christianity. There are many similarities between that era and ours. To discern them calls for considerable care and concentrated attention. We are beginning to discover a connection between the launching of the Church nineteen hundred years ago and the end of a road that we now seem to have reached. The validity of historic ecclesiastical structures (and all that goes with them) is now open to question. That validity seems certain to vanish. The Church, as we know it, was always subject to rapid changes and divisions, yet it has nevertheless, at any rate over the last fifteen hundred years, had a discernible inner and outer unitary structure. The question as to whether this Church can survive into the future has only now become a radical reality.

Is it sufficient to pull down a structure that will no longer serve and to erect a new one with the old and well tried bricks? Is rejuvenation all that is needed, modernization, reform? If so, no one surely would wish to get in the way. Or must the Church abandon the idea of building on its heritage and embark on a new, unpredictable adventure, accepting suppositions with indeterminable consequences?

'A Christianity that appeared can also disappear.' It may begin to dawn on us that we cannot begin to think in terms less radical than this proposition of a Dutch religious philosopher. The changes in our world are so radical that the traditional efforts to make reforms are wholly inadequate to meet today's real need. A touch of make-up will not suffice. The old bottles are no good for the new wine. Something unparalleled is in the process of happening. We cannot remain unaffected by it, the same people that we were yesterday.

It is fashionable to speak of our era as 'post-Christian'. This idea put forward by Hoekendijk is neither a complaint nor an accusation. It is simply a negative way of describing a state of affairs which has inherent in it a hidden *kairos* which we should discover. The proposition really arises out of our wanting to know whether we are right in trying to discover whether anything like a 'post-ecclesiastical Church' has begun to emerge. Perhaps Christendom is heading for a second *exodus*. Just as the Jews have abandoned Judaism and the heathens their paganism, so, maybe, we shall need to abandon our Christianity *in order to become Christians*. Perhaps we shall discover in the rapid social change of our time not only an end but also the beginnings of a new Christianity which we have not hitherto been able to discern. Perhaps the post-religious, the post-ecclesiastical age will once more be a New Testament age. I say 'perhaps' because these are open questions, observations and hopes and it would be improper to pretend that they were developed ideas or visions, let alone that they constituted a specific plan.

Dietrich Bonhoeffer is far too often and far too superficially quoted, either approvingly or disapprovingly, when this theme is under discussion. If we are prepared to cut through the surfeit of stereotyped views of both his admirers and his critics in order to penetrate to the man himself, there are inescapable surprises in store for us. It is the very open-endedness, the incompleteness, the biographical limitation of his work that makes it so attractive and stimulating. What 'religion-less Christianity' would look like, what form it would take, was the substance of his meditation in prison. He gave no answer. He was in no position to. Neither are we. But we can continue along the road that Bonhoeffer and others have begun to tread, instead of doing what is happening all along the line, seeking refuge in patterns of life and thought which we defend all the more vehemently as we become aware that we wear them like garments which even our friends know to be out of date. They are like ruins that can be admired but not inhabited.

In the light of our recognition of a 'world come of age which puts an end to a false image of God and clears the decks for a biblical God who attains a position of power and influence by virtue of his very powerlessness', we should take courage to enter into a new relationship with God, accepting the speed at which he moves, accepting his mode of entry into history, being ready to learn our lessons from him. When men are deprived of a particular mode of thought they tend to imagine that they have lost hold upon God. But perhaps it is not God who is lost but only a way of thinking about him, of imagining him. It is the objectivized God of the theologians and philosophers who is lost from sight along with the image of the world of which he was thought to be the mainspring. Atheism is a natural corollary of theism. The one presupposes the other. It is only in the light of the classical *proofs* of the existence of God that the current *denials* of his existence make any sense. The one is logically consequent upon the other. In fact we are confronted not so much with denials of *God's* existence as with denials of *proofs* for God.

But man's relation to God is too elemental a process to be subject to proofs of God's existence or to denials of these proofs. We have forgotten that. We have obscured the relationship between God and man by theologizing it. To realize that every breath we take is an expression of a relationship to God, apparently calls for a radical stripping down of our doctrines and images of God. As though this relationship to God depended on religious reflection and speculation! The metaphysical concept of God in its various forms and popularizations has unobtrusively, yet irrevocably, ceased to be valid and so, along with it, has the allegedly immutable prerequisite for human existence. The facts of modern life have swept all this away.

In the face of this loss, Christians and non-Christians share a common bewilderment. At the same time they share a common hope. Together they can catch a glimpse of how he has triumphed by the destruction of his own images. We cannot capture God in metaphors and symbols, in rites and formulations; it is he who takes hold of us, always anew, never the same twice, always taking us by surprise. *And this is called history.* History is God, daring us to keep up with him. God is never a God of yesterday. Wherever we go, wherever we look, God is always there ahead of us. And he comes to meet us. He is present in a form of his own choosing. His own self-determination puts paid to all attempts on our part to define him. God is never in our hands. His presence is a latent presence. Jesus frequently vanished from human sight after he had come very close to people, after becoming their neighbour.

The more abstract and unhistorical our images of

God have been and the more skilfully we have depicted God as the Being on which all existence depends, as the infinite on whom all finitude depends, the more we have felt justified in giving expression to his dominance over the universe. Yet, *where God is, there relativity is also.* If we still feel inclined to speak of our experience of God, then we can only do so in the context of relativity, a context springing from relationship. For God, all that lives is basically historical and so even death is relativized. Absolute concepts of God are therefore much more inadequate than partial ones.

It bears thinking about that the disciples of Jesus were thought to be atheists. They trusted a God whom it was possible to kill. The concept that 'God is dead' is not just a creation of the nineteenth century. Nor is it just part of the litany of so-called modern man. It is a New Testament concept. All that has happened is that this idea has, with immense impact, become a world-wide experience. What the theologians have always claimed has now become a self-evident fact of everyday experience: God has not been hewn from the wood of this world. When Karl Rahner speaks of 'troubled atheists' he surely has in mind the connection between them and the dereliction of Good Friday that emerges from the biblical texts and that springs from an understanding of the God-forsakenness of the world. The Son of God did not even leave a relic behind. When the women came to anoint his body they found an empty grave and were told that God is not to be found where the religious expect to find him.

'My God, why hast thou forsaken me?' That is not just an exclamation. It is a characterization of the situation of Christ, Christians and Christianity. But the disciples set about proclaiming the absurd: Jesus is the Christ, the Crucified is the Risen, the Dead is the Living, the Abased is the Exalted. In defeat he is victorious! As a child he is the Lord, as a king he is a servant! The contradiction in this message is the news of the New Testament. God helps men not on account of his power but because he is weak. He who is far off is near. His life is in his death. His revelation is in his hiddenness. We can neither take charge of him nor eliminate him. We can neither identify him nor tie him down; and yet it is exclusively in the reality of the world that we can approach him. Only in the midst of the world is it possible to witness to him. Only when we seriously come to terms with his absence is he present. For, as Bonhoeffer remarked, the God who 'is there' does not exist. God tells us that we must live in his presence as men who exist without God. Bonhoeffer has been accused of clinging to a theology of Good Friday on account of this paradox. But is there any way of transcending this paradox; is there any way in which we can speak of the presence of God other than by speaking of the absent God?

Simone Weil, the unbaptized Christian, was able to say that given two people, both without experience of God, the one who denies God is the closer to him. Her life was a demonstration to Christians of solidarity with men unaccompanied by every routine relationship with

God. With utmost rigour she forwent every religious practice, every comfort that might ensue. She showed what it means to live as though God did not exist (*etsi deus non daretur*). This should not be in any way minimized. The attempt to smuggle God back into the structures and ways of life of today's world must be resisted. But we may well ask whether Simone Weil's experience does not make it possible for us to understand St Paul's sermon about the God of the godless, as probably no previous generation could. Is this godlessness not the prerequisite for a totally fresh encounter with the God of scripture? The perplexed affirmation and the dedicated readiness to live without God has inherent within it a trust that is without guarantees but that is eminently practicable and characteristic of our nature. There is implied a trust that God is at work: *etsi deus daretur*. We must take risks.

Secular Godliness

I am sure that some path must be found between godless man and man clinging to God. They are both misguided. And, what is even more significant, they are two different forms of the same disease. If clinging to a definable deity as the highest form of 'insurance policy' is illusory, so is today's fashionable idea that God can be simply ignored. These are complementary illusions, much more closely related than appears at first sight. They have a common root. The one stands by the world, ignoring God, the other by God, ignoring the world. They are supplementary and must be confronted by us with a *living secularism*, a relationship with the world that is true to its nature, yet that does not turn it into a new absolute, a relationship that neither shuts God in nor shuts him out but that allows the world to express its own autonomy, to be itself. The true nature of creation must be revealed and not perverted. The world was not made to be despised, overlooked or rejected. It was made to be fully discovered. And our relationship to God depends on our relationship with the world just as much as our relationship to the world depends on our relationship to God.

Blumhardt said that a conversion to Christ must be followed by a conversion to the world. He was not speaking simply of individuals. He was thinking historically. It seems clear that the whole of Christendom today needs to be converted to the world. The Church must in fact *become* world, somewhat as the Word became flesh. What this process will look like defies systematic definition. We need examples of wide-awake, honest and self-critical Christians, men neither of yesterday nor of tomorrow, men who are prepared to take the greatest possible risks today. We need examples of a new, courageous and secular form of godliness that is open to the apparently undesirable, that is prepared to sit lightly to past principles, that rejects any ideas that prejudge an issue. We need Christians who will, without concern for the future, experiment in faith and love with the present.

What religious labels men have is immaterial. But the effects of what they believe is all important. The fruits of faith are the trade-marks of religion. The practice of Christianity does not permit of an evacuation of the world but rather demands its penetration. Flight into the beyond, however conceived, is ruled out. Instead we are committed to taking risks here and now. Far from encouraging 'cultivation' of one's own spiritual life, true religion commits us to life for others. There is no room in true piety for spiritual parochialism but only for an open universality of outlook. Its hallmarks are accuracy and reliability rather than vagueness and easy comfort. It calls for a readiness to ask questions rather than an attitude of knowing all the answers. Instead of—as the persistent critics claim—being no more than a compensation for our inadequacies, and one that has good cause to fear the psychoanalyst, religion must be an adventure of Christian existence in the world, never isolated, but right at the heart of the facts and problems, the decisions and disappointments of modern life, bringing them all into play critically and therapeutically, being both a challenge and a liberating influence.

In his comedy *Don Juan or the Love of Geometry* Max Frisch writes: 'Beyond the incense, where there is clarity, light and no more obscurity, revelations begin . . . only the sober man can begin to sense what is holy; all else is mere tinsel, not worth wasting time on.' Or, as Robert Musil puts it: 'The mysterious only holds good if it can stand up to the precision demanded by an engineer.' In Bonhoeffer's words: 'A "pious" scientist or doctor is a hybrid.'

It is not a matter of pleading for some uni-dimensional, *simpliciste* enlightenment. These quotations merely clarify the radical transformation that has taken place. We are left alone to cope with the accessible world. Its mysteries, the inaccessible in the accessible, will only unfold themselves if we show competence and are disciplined enough to know the limits of our own capacity. We must be fully open to the world to which we have access, to its promise and its dangers. We must be prepared to plumb its depths, and to welcome the insight it offers: that despite the rationality of all processes, many of life's most significant events are beyond our understanding. That must be the nature of our piety. At one and the same time it renounces both more and less.

This piety will no longer primarily be able to base itself on our childlike dependence. Rather it will come alive in active and adult co-operation with God. Luther speaks of the *co-operatores dei*. The expression of this co-operation does not permit of the banning of God to a transcendental sphere; it does not put God in a world of his own, but assumes that God is to be found wherever he chooses to reveal himself. Where? In the world, not the world on Sunday but the ordinary workaday world. This form of piety would, in its secular realization, be a sharing of the way of the cross, a participation in God's ceaseless work of creation and redemption.

Our sights, then, are not so much set upwards as forwards. We are less concerned with achievements that need to be safeguarded, than with projects to be carried out, at risk. Teilhard de Chardin tended to regard pessimism as a more insidious poison than atheism. Eager expectancy is *the* realm of meeting with a God who still has plans for the world and who seeks fellow workers in creating the new universe, the 'new *oikumene*'. Because we believe that God exists neither in nor above the world but rather *for* it and *with* it, our relationship to him must primarily be one of being his companions, suffering with him and sharing him with others. The will to keep in step with God, to be in harmony with God, to agree to what he expects us to do and to accept what he does not want us to do, to accept what is ours and what remains unique to him: that is faith. It is a way of life rather than a dogmatic system.

The piety of our time is no longer to be vertical but horizontal in its emphasis. It is an adventure, a risk, an experiment. It has many surprises in store for us but it will also bring with it new certainties, new attitudes with which we shall find it quite possible to live.

We are not really searching for new images of God but for fresh understanding of his action and purpose. History has given us a distorted vision of these. Our experiences are likely to be more concrete, more in the Old Testament tradition, and therefore less easily turned to our own use, less religious, more flexible, less reducible to our patterns than the conventional religious experience to which we have grown accustomed. There are straws in the wind in the ecumenical sphere but also in the realms of art, technology and politics—in the endless variety of our real relationships with men and with things. *The world is full of God's undiscovered intentions.* Today's world is full of unexpected appeals to a genuine piety which will take its demands seriously and seek to answer its questions, which will engender confidence and courage in an open encounter with reality.

One might well draw together all the questions raised by the present crisis of Christianity by defining our relationship, in faith, to the world. The traditional scheme of things that is based on a dialectic of Christian solidarity with the world and of Christian dissociation from it, will no longer suffice in the light of our present appreciation of what the world is like. The Bible contains such a plethora of secular experience (and I do not merely mean reflected experience) that traditional systematic teaching about a living world of history is woefully inadequate in that context. For Israel the world is not static but dynamic. We are once more beginning to think in terms of a dynamic historical process. It falls to us to work out a totally new appreciation of the world which takes the dynamism of biblical truth into account and relates it to our experience of real life. We must be bold enough to venture far beyond the accustomed and traditional categories of thought to the vision of a yet to be written but urgently needed chapter of theological history. This task can only be accomplished in a dialogue that crosses the frontiers of intellectual disciplines, of Christian denominations, of religions and races, ideologies and continents.

Since the beginnings of Church history when Christians refused to pay religious homage to the Emperor, they have been known by their *No*. Today the stock types and patterns of Christian refusal are in large measure ineffective and often made to no purpose. What we should not want to see is that the Christian conscientious objector should become a Yes-man. A mistaken attitude would then merely be replaced by an apparent change. The *no* to the world backed by the authority of knowledge, the *no* without which the world would be like an unsalted dish, this *no* will only carry weight if there is a fundamental *yes* at its heart, a *yes* springing from the deepest fraternal partnership with all other human beings no matter how different in outlook, faith or colour. Christians must be in a position to demonstrate that even through their critique, and their anger, their faith has something positive to offer the world and its people in the future. Failing that, Christians will rightly be suspected of being utterly irrelevant.

The Redemption of History

The laboratory, or better still the home of faith, the only place where it can function, is the world, the one reality in which we live, struggle, suffer, die—history itself and not just some abstracted slice of it. The world is not the antithesis of faith but its subject matter. Faith is committed to the service of the world and cannot pass it by. Without the world there can be no faith. Faith determines the nature of the world. Faith penetrates and illuminates, sees that 'the quality of the world is rooted in the joy of God' (Calvin). He is both guarantor and healer of the world and the fact that he is widely held to be an opponent or even saboteur of the world points to an unbiblical and heretical attitude to the world on the part of most Christians and of the churches. The main function of faith is not to condemn but create. The 'great hope' of faith is both a stimulant and a corrective to the 'little hopes' of man's personal and communal life. In its joyful expectancy faith triumphs over the old and gathers in the new. Faith does not annul creation. It allows it to happen and makes history of it. That is its real function. Without faith there would be no history. Faith sets us free from slavishly normative ties to the past, sets us free from powerful entanglements with the standards and sins of yesterday and makes possible true openness to tomorrow's world. The forgiveness, the absolution which we accept in faith fills us with confidence in the future and is thereby instrumental in constituting history.

Faith takes the world, as creation and history, under its wing, giving it purpose and direction, confidence and openness. Contrary to certain appearances, faith upholds the created and historical order. Faith co-operates in the bitter struggle to win the world back as God's creation and to set it free in its historic role. Faith, then, does not ebb out of the world, it rather confirms it. Faith does not merely suffer the world, it also transforms it. It exists—in the words of Matthias Claudius— not in abstraction, not in its own right, as if it could be abstracted and gazed at; it exists in concrete form, in the midst of the world, with a positive overall effect on daily life. Faith becomes incarnate reality, involved in events in such a way that Christ reveals the reality of God within the reality of the world. According to the most ancient theological tradition God is unthinkable without the world and spirit is unthinkable without the body. Only in the awareness of the physical do we approach the singular nature of God. Had God not seen salvation in terms of physical life he would not have become man. It is in the very act of becoming man that he remains divine. He wills his divinity to be humanity.

That is why it is impossible to talk of salvation in the abstract. It only begins to make sense in terms of its healing consequences. You cannot speak of salvation theologically without also talking about it politically. The enthusiasts, the atheists and the Christians who seek to put the world to rights, men like Blumhardt and Brecht, Reinhold Schneider and Camus have seen this point. Only in this context do these men have something in common. There is much that might be said of them; the most important is this: they are rooted in and reviving a tradition which is as old as theology itself, one which today has radically new implications.

Faithlessness can be recognized by the fact that it divides up reality. It gambles away and undermines the fact of the Incarnation. Faith, on the other hand, is the extension of the Incarnation. Faith does not immunize man against being a child of this world or sterilize his secular existence; rather it gives that existence a new dimension and enables man to respond to the world as he should. To let the world be world is the way of letting God be God. The world, as scripture says, 'loves the darkness more than the light', and this is echoed with strange passion by the religious and the irreligious alike. Surely not even the enthusiast can doubt it! But faith does not leave the world to put up its shutters. Faith enlightens the world. Faith sets limits on the world's rebellion, condemns its self-glorification, confronts its illusions with realism, its ideologies with an untrammelled mind. Faith is a stumbling block to the world's security, confronts its narrow vision with universal appeal, displaces its maladjustment with sober self-knowledge.

In the man of faith, God enters into the real world. This is not careerism. This is a way that leads to, rather than away from, the pitfalls of history. God chooses this world and not some other. We are saved *in* this world, not *from* it; *for* this world and not *against* it. His is the world that is not his. He has not merely touched it at a tangent, but has come powerless into the world; *the lamb* of God. Any sacrifice that does not tread this path of pro-existence—of life for others—bereft of all power, is the most terrible rebellion against God, committed in God's name, no matter how perfect is the liturgy with which it is celebrated. God has submitted himself totally to the conditions of true secularity, even to death on the cross which put the final seal on the here-and-now of God's world.

The death of Jesus is this world's death. To kill him is suicide. Yet over and over again the world and its people commit suicide. But God raised his son on the third day. This fact is not less significant, not less important historically than the crucifixion. The world can never be the same again. It has changed because *God has entered into the world, without being absorbed by it.* From that moment everything had changed. God had established a relationship with the world which would lead to a new relationship between man and the world. This changed relationship of man to creation demands ceaseless change in man's world.

Because of certain historical facts—the facts of the life of *the* man, Jesus of Nazareth—a new truth has been implanted by God in history. Its publication is what we call Gospel. The gospels are the literary records of the verbal reports of the proclamation and effect of the Gospel. The gospels are not the Gospel. But without the gospels there is no way of our knowing the Gospel. We depend on the information they contain. It is not for us to retell the gospels as though this were merely historical narrative. The Gospel calls for a type of reconstruction that is not merely concerned with the past but that opens doors into the future and does it in terms of the present. In this process the news of the Gospel is both information and interpretation. The Gospel of the risen and glorified Christ, the Lord of all men and ages, comes to us through the historical narrative. This narrative is not mere reporting. The facts demand to be preached: they make it imperative to proclaim that God's truth is here revealed in history and that his will triumphs through history. This news is not about an event, it is the event itself. It cannot really be defined

in terms of its content but only in terms of its consequences. The man who has understood the news is
gratified, he can relax, he has acquired certainty. He
is at peace in himself. It is not merely that something
. is reported, but rather that something is achieved. This
news does not depend on its own merit as do other
historical narratives. This is history in the present tense
and indeed in the future. Its effects are never-ending. It
is constantly active and releases energy. It creates new
circumstances wherever it 'happens'. It communicates
more than knowledge and cannot simply be culled from
the world's cumulative store simply to give straightforward answers as part of the normal historical repertoire.
Yet the news of the Gospel cannot be isolated from the
physical world without which it would have no reality.
The facts neither confirm nor supplement secular history, they do not merely verify or add a little colour.
The facts bring to life something new, decisive, unlikely,
unknown; something essential, hopeful, something
grounded in the future. Something *that makes Easter real.*
Easter gives the world the power to transcend itself, not
in order to become something alien, but in order to be
its true self. This process is bound to leave traces that
are somewhat unclear. But anyone in touch with the
real world will inevitably come across these traces.

Since these events the reality of Easter has become
secular reality. Salvation is now part of history. The one
reality cannot be abstracted from the other. They
depend on one another for veracity. There is tension
between the two, rather than harmony, they are corre-

lative, but there is no dualism, nor legitimate separateness. It is only possible to understand *both* realities if they are seen as *one*. Their integration is part of the process of faith. *He who alone is reality*, God made man, creates and liberates, sustains and tests *what is real alone*. Without him there is only unreality.

For that reason there can be nothing more terrible than a belief in Easter that ignores the world, that impatiently 'emigrates' and seeks to exist without identifying with the world. The Church, in conflict with its own better insights, has for centuries often succumbed to the strange error of believing in a disincarnate Easter. The Church is nullified by the way it believed in the Resurrection. The Church has placed a barrier between God (and itself) and the world. This schism, with all that it implies, can no longer be maintained. In this fact lies the hope of our age.

3

CHRISTIANS AND NON-CHRISTIANS

Dedication to the Gospel must always lead to a new and living sense of brotherhood with all men. Yet our tired segments of the Church, burdened by the whole weight of their history, try to take men captive by shutting them off in a special compartment from the rest of mankind. All too often the churches are saddled with reactionary views, rooted in the past and limping along behind the times. We accept this state of affairs all too readily, generally without admitting it to ourselves. We allow ourselves to be caught up in a Christian environment that we find congenial and in the process create a ghetto of like-minded people who are quite unmindful of the real world.

ROGER SCHUTZ

Dialogue, not Assertion

No one today is likely to turn a hair at the assertion that a Christian polity (*corpus christianum*) has no future. Yet the ideas that go with this concept are far from outmoded. In fact they constitute the substance of most of the current views of what the Church is all about.

74

They also determine the actual shape of our main denominations. Yet in tomorrow's world there is just no place for the idea of a Christian polity.

The world has shrunk, has become one world. It is a complex constellation in which everything is related and interdependent. Continents come closer to each other. Cultures and civilizations become more and more alike. Technology is the great standardizer. It is more potent than divisive traditions. It breaks down differences and distances and brings similarities and agreements to the fore even at points where deep ideological and political divisions constitute a threat to peace.

Yet it would be wrong to assume that the world has solely become more unified. It is also going through a process of greater stratification. Not only has the world become more homogeneous, it has concurrently become more pluralistic. There is no longer a generally accepted system of thought or conduct. Men who were once fenced off from each other now come face to face. No nation, no race, no religion can go on existing as though it were possible to escape comparison and involvement with others. Self-assertion is no longer effective. It has become necessary to justify one's existence. Everyone has become a challenge to everyone else. Everything is open to question. It is no longer possible to take anything—not even one's own life—for granted. The pluralism with which the world now has to cope is also something with which every individual will have to come to terms.

In this situation it is not a great synthesis that is

needed. No institution or philosophy is called for that is going to embrace all the world's divergent forces and powers, removing every present tension. No universally valid system of truth and order based on our traditions of classical antiquity is called for today. What is needed is freedom, and the capacity to bring about an untrammelled meeting of minds where, while maintaining one's own position, one will be led to accept global terms of reference which will make it possible to think and plan boldly and experimentally for the good of all mankind. Such dialogue would need to lead to a worldwide feeling of solidarity. If we fail to achieve such solidarity there is good reason to think that we might well destroy the world.

Tomorrow's social structures, which rule out the possibility of any sort of exclusiveness, constitute an inescapable challenge for Christianity. Nowhere in this world is there going to be room for any sort of individual or corporate exclusiveness. In no situations will Christians be the sole factor. Yet there are always likely to be *some* Christians involved in every situation. Christians will live among non-Christians. The Christian polity will give way to the Church in dispersion. The Church is not man's home but rather the salt of the earth. It is characterized not by a cathedral but by a tent. The Church lives as a scattered minority in an alien environment that at times constitutes a threat to its survival. Dialogue displaces assertion, encounter displaces conversion, an offer displaces a demand, the role of the priest gives way to that of the Samaritan.

The conditions under which Christianity is going to have to exist in tomorrow's world are becoming increasingly clear. A very sketchy outline should suffice here. At the beginning of this century half of the world's people were Christian. Today there are eight hundred million Christians and one thousand five hundred million non-Christians. Christians make up only one-third of the total. By the end of the century there is likely to be an increase to four thousand million people. The non-Christian peoples are increasing at a breathtaking pace. There is no hope of Christianity keeping up with this rate of increase. There are still some Christian strongholds. The Christians have wealth on their side. The Christian third of the world is, by and large, that part which does not merely live well, but lives in superabundance. The future is likely to see an intensification of this disproportionate state of affairs. The rich will get richer. They are likely to raise their standard of living to a point with which they will no longer be able to cope. There are already indications that comfortable western society is rapidly becoming one of the most onerous forms of life mankind has yet devised. Meanwhile two thirds of mankind are heading for even greater deprivation and poverty. Unless the unexpected happens, they will fall victim to the inescapable stresses of industrialization and secularization.

In this situation of intolerable disequilibrium the strength of Christendom is likely to prove its weakness. How can it convincingly champion the poor without sharing their poverty? How is it to be recognized as a prototype of what the world needs, when it is either geared to a strategy of worldly success or to one of pious withdrawal linked to a hope of life to come? Where is the readiness to be spent unconditionally in the world's service? Christianity as at present constituted deepens the world's divisions rather than helping to heal them. It is incapable of plausibly demonstrating that what binds men together in one world is the fact of being challenged and confronted by one God. The preaching of the one God has helped to bring about the one world. It is the prophecy of the Last Judgment, where *all* men meet, that has given our world the vision of a universal humanity. Eschatology and universality go together. But Christendom has not been able to cope with the implications. Its true function in today's world remains unfulfilled. Christians should be signposts to the unification of mankind. There are indeed some manifestations of such ecumenicity, the products of the world's inescapable demands. But our established churches are far from being caught up in this process.

Confessionally divided Christendom is incapable of responding to the questions today being put to the Church. It lacks a vision of worldwide responsibility which is surely the unfulfilled prerequisite for the interest in the Church that is so often demanded of non-Christians. The Church in its denominations has learnt to live with its divisions. The various groups have even ceased to speak each other's language. Despite an astonishingly spontaneous will to unity, the churches still fall back on pathos, taking strange delight in their mutual love-hate relationships. The differences between the confessions go deep. They reflect basically different attitudes and ideas on why the Church exists. Conventional analyses will not get to the heart of these differences nor can they be understood simply by a process of using traditional definitions. Not only differing dogmatic conceptions are at issue but opposing ideas of what the Christian life implies. Ecclesiastical terminology reduces complex situations to formulae which are valid enough but which fail to speak to our situation. There is much to be said for the writing of a phenomenology of the Christian confessions. It would need to embrace art and politics, aesthetics and everyday customs. Somehow the fact that Catholics, Orthodox and Anglicans worship differently from Christians of the Reformed tradition is all tied up with the fact that they look at life differently, have a different sense of humour, argue differently; in fact their minds work differently.

Reinhold Schneider—son of a catholic mother and a protestant father—described the deep abyss between the different traditions (occasioned mainly by non-theological factors) as follows: 'My life was a "thirty years' war", the armies go into battle, and I live on both sides of the battlefield and, as far as I can see, understand the opponent every bit as well as myself. I am secure in my own position but quite unable to refute that of my opponent.'

This is not just a general dilemma. It is the expression of a deep change that is taking place. Men are beginning to live on both sides of the battlefield. Friendships which transcend confessional barriers are becoming more and more common. Common action which creates solidarity with one's brother in the other camp is part of the surprising experience of our generation. The many mixed marriages are not particularly concerned with episcopal pronouncements and pastoral letters. And that isn't just because ecclesiastical authority has lost a good deal of the respect once due to it, but rather because denominational differences have increasingly ceased to make sense. The official differences between the churches are no longer the real ones. The frontiers no longer run along the traditional lines drawn on the confessional maps. Denominational terminology is still in current use, but it has long since lost its effectiveness. It can no longer adequately describe the nature and effect of Christian realities in the twentieth century. Facts reduce traditional differences almost to irrelevance. The confessions of Christendom in some respects are more like façades than houses, more like museums than homes. History has overtaken them, reduced former alternatives to insignificance. True, it is still possible to make something of these differences, but it cuts no ice. Perhaps instead of dwelling on old controversies, we should simply dare to affirm that they have lost all substance.

In Europe, where the confessions were born, they still have their part to play. History cannot be undone. Why should it be? But in Asia, and not only there, these differences are offensive and strictly speaking meaningless. They have no roots in history, are foreign and are unacceptable. For a long time the attempt was made to export our quarrels, to transplant them into Asian soil. What nonsense this is has now become clear, not without repercussions on our own religious situation. It is beginning to dawn on us that we have entered a post-confessional epoch with which we are ill-equipped to deal.

Confessionalism could be the formal expression of an organized obstruction to *living-out* the Christian integration that has in fact already taken place. Despite its continued existence, there is such a thing as living ecumenism which constitutes an ecclesiological reality, however little that reality can be fitted into the thought-structures of denominational division. Willem Visser 't Hooft has rightly asked whether it is not better to live with a reality that defies definition than with a definition that is devoid of reality. Many of the churches' most exciting experiments in thought and action have no denominational label. They span or transcend the churches, are at one and the same time committed to them and free of them. Simone Weil, whose life posed the acute problem of Christian existence outside the structure of the Church, felt that she had moved from Judaism to Christianity, but not to one of its segments. It is easy to show up her error, but that fails to do justice to the challenge of her life, which is surely a reflection of God's challenge to his Church today.

Does that mean, then, that we commit ourselves to a

sort of Esperanto-Christianity? Do we simply fall into each others' arms and shout Hallelujah? Do we merge into one great new confession? To do any of these things would not only be unrealistic but against the true spirit of ecumenism. The advocates of the 'great new church' are generally those who want a strong and disciplined re-creation of Christendom, a new *corpus christianum* as a bulwark against a dechristianized world. This tendency to create a Christian power-structure is the more dangerous because it is championed in the 'highest' quarters as a weapon both of offence and defence against political atheism. But it is an open, not a closed type of Christianity that is needed today. It is not power we need, but spiritual authority. We need no bulwarks. We need a Church without privileges, that embarks on no crusades.

Our traditional churches cannot simply shake off their history. What they cannot do is to expect others, to whom their structures and formulations make no sense, to accept these as binding. They must come to terms with the fact that the experiences which they had turned into absolutes have to a considerable extent been shown to be geographically, sociologically and psychologically limited. They must be prepared to enter into bold dialogue, to make sacrifices, to concede that they have not arrived at finality but are still in a process of 'becoming'. Dialogue implies a practice of the ecumenical virtue of getting to the roots of one's own position, yet not maintaining it stubbornly and without charity. Ecumenical dialogue implies a readiness to be put right and to be enriched thereby. There can be no winner or loser of such discussion, only transformed participants, companions on the way. Truth is never the victim of such dialogue. On the contrary, a radical search for it makes the abandonment of self-righteous adherence to one's own position inevitable. An insistence on maintaining truth can only promote and never endanger the unity of the Church. *Yet truth itself is rooted in dialogue.* Truth only has a chance to come alive in the exchange of conversation. It cannot be promoted by monologues.

The denominations have been so busy propagating their version of truth that mutual knowledge has not gone very far. It is high time to take the risk of meeting. It is an adventure; to embark on it is bound to bring surprises. One's own views are hardly likely to be rubber-stamped by others. What we must hope for is a deeper mutual understanding. Favourite ideas, cherished hopes and much loved customs will need to go by the board. Oversimplifications, ideals and images will all need to finish up in the melting-pot of dialogue. This will by no means eliminate differences, but these may re-emerge in more genuine and realistic form. Take them out of their historical context, and the conflicts— to the surprise of all the antagonists—may take on completely new contours. The 'line up' may look quite different. It is not indifference that is called for, but openness, not superficiality, but a readiness to get to the roots, not a general levelling down, but clearer definition, not an ignoring of differences, but a critical examination of their validity. We must have courage to transcend our fear-ridden narrowness. That is the purpose of encounter. Only from an untrammelled position can the right of particularity be maintained. Ideally, we should aspire to the freedom to live on in our confessional structures *as though they did not exist.*

Ecumenism, rightly understood, does not imply Christianity without confessions. It makes possible the recognition that *the Church* only becomes real through the complementary existence of *the churches.* The Church's multiplicity is in itself neither good nor bad, it is simply its particular nature. It is in dialogue, even in hard-fought debates, between the churches that they become the Church. In the mutual giving that dialogue implies the churches can come to a realization of their own nature which transcends the limited self-evaluation of a church which claims to be *the* Church and which attributes to itself total authority and even juridical primacy. 'Every church has something that the others need, and every church needs what the others can give. The life of the various churches is increasingly being shaped by giving content to this insight.' So says a message of the East Asian Christian Conference. It is no longer possible to be a Christian or to be a Christian Church without the other Christians and churches.

Paul S. Minear has pointed out that the New Testament uses eighty different terms to describe what we call 'church'. All these words indicate the inadequacy of trying to reduce the Church to one description. The picture we are given of the Church in the New Testament contains all the tensions and contradictions, all the uncertainties, all the illogicalities that we see in the modern Church. Ernst Käsemann says that the New Testament Church is like the Church today: 'At best, it was an ecumenical confederation without a World Council of Churches.' There can be no thought of any 'unbroken unity of New Testament ecclesiology'. From the start, there have been varying forms of Christianity and alternative types of Church and theology. The early churches in fact maintained their position through debate and constant delimiting of their positions. It is therefore not the variety but the exclusiveness of the churches, their competing with one another, that stands in the way of true ecumenicity. The uniting of church structures does not correspond to New Testament demands; unity without uniformity does. The Church owes a pluralistic world a many-sided witness.

The overcoming of confessional differences, the creation of one human structure, will not establish the unity of the Church. To imagine otherwise would be to confuse unity with uniformity. Unity is by its nature many-sided and pluralistic. Unity cannot be possessed but only achieved. It is not static but dynamic. It is not assured simply by the fact that the churches are at one. Unity does not primarily become articulate in the discourse that the churches have with each other, but rather in their converse with the world. The unity of the Church is in its essential nature not manifested by the

conversations the churches and denominations have
with each other, but in the meeting of Christians with
non-Christians. The question which the ecumenical
movement must answer is not: 'What is the true
church?' but rather: 'How can the churches of the
world make the truth known?'

The unity of the Church derives from the universality
of its mission. The apostolic nature of the Church,
directing its message to the whole world, is both the
sign and the reality of its unity. As the people of God the
Church heralds and embodies the future of the peoples
of the earth. The content of ecumenicity is the *oikumene*,
the whole of humanity, to all the ends of the earth and
to the end of time. Where the commitment and hope of
Christians believing in the one God becomes identified
with the commitment and hope of one world, the one
true Church becomes incarnate, beyond all structures,
but in and through the many churches.

What is Solidarity?

Is it just a slogan? In the course of a discussion I learnt
that the word does not occur in the New Testament,
that it has no biblical status. The objection to solidarity,
to identification of the Christian with the world, was
hammered home by asking what the point of solidarity
with the Nazis would have been in Hitler's Germany.
My response was to reply with a question: What would
have happened if the Christians of Germany had reso-
lutely followed the example of a few non-Christian
intellectuals in Paris and elsewhere who identified them-

selves with the outcast and persecuted Jews by wearing, as these had to, a yellow star? Through every Christian who would have been a Jew to the Jews (with all that that entailed), history might have been able to take a different course. When Pastor Paul Schneider went to his death in opposition to Nazi rule he had not ceased to identify with the world. In fact he had declared war on those who had sought to usurp the power of God. The fact that the New Testament does not explicitly speak of solidarity does not suffice to rule out this concept.

Solidarity is not one of several possible modes of human conduct for believers. It is their essential *raison d'être*. Eugen Rosenstock-Huessy wrote of the *incognito* existence of the Christian. We remain anonymous, do not choose names for ourselves. They will be given us by others in the light of what we are. The man on the road to Jericho who falls among thieves suddenly becomes more than a Samaritan. He becomes a neighbour. This sort of anonymity has nothing to do with secrecy, with the denial of one's identity. It does imply a readiness to give up any particularly circumscribed or privileged existence. The Christian, as Luther said, should be without any particular mark of identity, not distinguishable from others, with no personal marks of distinction. This anonymity is not a matter of tactics, not camouflage, not an accommodating masquerade. It goes to the heart of things. Being a Christian means being human.

The nameless Christian is the Christian who identifies

87

with others. God became man and thereby put an end
to a legalistic religion, keeping its distance. The believer
cannot be exempted from the human solidarity which is
both the product and the challenge of freedom. The
Christian is called to life in the world which knows no
limits in its commitment to others. Religion by its very
nature calls for a certain dissociation from life, a going
apart, a disengagement; Pharisaism, if you like. Faith,
on the other hand, is a prerequisite for true solidarity.
And faith brings it to fulfilment. As faith does not permit
of a distinction between the sacred and the secular, man
is left free to serve, untrammelled by religious or cere-
monial limitations, uniquely free to be at the disposal
of others.

Solidarity is anything but the artificial creation of an
insincere attitude. For Christians to be as worldly as
possible is no way of achieving this identification with
the world. By demonstrating that we are 'with it', we
fall far short of really being part of today's world. We
are in the habit of speaking of modern man (whatever
that may mean) as though we ourselves were not
modern men. Every attempt at identification is under
these circumstances bound to be something of a propa-
gandistic fancy dress parade. However much we put on
our red hoods we cannot in the end get away from the
fact that, as in the fairy tale, pretending to be grand-
mother does not change our nature or our dishonourable
intentions. To change the imagery, the modern man we
are trying to get alongside strongly resents us in the role
of pied piper.

True solidarity cannot be explained at all in terms of making ourselves like others. It is neither a means nor an end. To begin with it is simply the renunciation of the immodest attitude of keeping our distance, the shedding of our wretched and irritating arrogance which always makes out that we are somehow a cut above others, an arrogance that in fact springs from a feeling of inferiority.

Solidarity or identification with others must spring from solidarity with oneself. One of the reasons that faith today has lost the power of speech, has lost effectiveness, initiative and appeal is partly explained by the fact that those who profess this faith are no longer able to identify with themselves. They have lost touch with reality. In the process of practising their religion they have cut themselves off from the real world around them. They have become isolated and innoculated. They have accepted the drawing of a frontier between themselves and their fellow-men whose contemporaries, deep down in their hearts, they long to be. In fact Christians have become as strange to non-Christians as non-Christians are to Christians. Communication between them has been much more seriously disrupted than is generally assumed. The Church in the West has acquired an ingrained tendency to dissociate itself from its environment. This inability to identify with the world robs the Church of its authority. It leads to gnostic and docetic distortions of the Gospel. It signifies a disincarnate church.

The opposite of faith is not always disbelief or even

superstition. It may well be some form of orthodoxy or legalistic religion: by this I mean the confusion of faith with some definable doctrine or order to which ultimate value is imputed. In reality faith is *vita experimentalis* in the midst of the endless variety of our experience and of our perception in time and space and of our constant intercourse with man and creation. 'How long,' asks Hans Schmidt, 'must the biblical message be put forward as timeless, as standing outside history, how long formalized into an "eternal" posture before it brings on what is surely the gravest crisis in the history of Christianity, a crisis that is evident in the defensive posture with which the western churches seek to protect their values, their ideals, their creeds and their traditions? How long must the Gospel be held captive in a ghetto of confessional formulations and definitions of previous generations; how long has the overdue message that man should hear today been so silenced, that the relationship between alleged truth and experienced reality, the relationship between belief and experience appears to have become unbridgeable?'

This agonizing question is given literary expression in Reinhold Schneider's diary of a journey, *Winter in Wien*. Not by mere coincidence do we find him, the Franciscan, spending his last months talking to natural scientists, physicians, astronomers and physicists. Nor is it any coincidence that he had lost interest in contacts with clerics. What the churches stood for seemed to be just one more ideology, no doubt well meant, but in the last resort a discredited presentation of historically explicable opinions, judgments and interests. It amounted to an apologia for preconceptions which get between ourselves and what is new, unexpected and unknown.

Schneider, for the sake of the faith, confronted his own beliefs with an experience that ruthlessly robbed those beliefs of security. He squarely faced the facts of our time. He did not permit himself the luxury of claiming more than he could substantiate. He accepted the rigorous disciplines demanded by intellectual integrity. In apparently unconnected reflections and terse descriptive passages he spoke of the demise of the Christian piety of which previously he had not only approved, but of which he had been an outstanding exponent. He began to call in question glib talk of God the Father, facile belief in eternal life and piety that thoughtlessly disregarded the insights of science and technology. The unforeseen, the 'accidental', happened to Schneider. What had been the essence of his life became incidental and superfluous. He knew that in committing this to writing he was disappointing and disturbing many people who had trusted his words. Yet the two possible alternative courses seemed equally dishonest to him: either pretence at continuing security in the tradition or silence about his own significant experience. And so he spoke, spoke not only of what had become irrelevant but also of what he believed would become significant. Reinhold Schneider abandoned the security and certainty of a much loved and well proved way of life and thought. In a representative capacity he committed himself step by step to an open, free and insecure venture. 'Let us be on our way, not knowing our destination. Let us go simply to be on the way.'

In the light of this sort of emigration from traditional positions one might well ask what the Church would look like, were it to exist today in a state of spontaneity, untrammelled by convention. There seems no doubt that it would be utterly different from its present shape if it had the freedom to be a product of the conditions and needs of our time. It would be much more akin to its revolutionary beginnings nineteen hundred years ago. This is confirmed by a glance at a number of small Christian communities in Africa and Asia which to us appear to be depressingly small minorities in the midst of a non-Christian world, yet which reveal a much greater degree of vigour than our established ecclesiastical institutions.

It is little wonder that places like Agape, Taizé, Iona, Grandchamp—and to an even greater degree East Harlem and *servezio cristiano* in Riesi—have remarkable appeal. This is equally true of the Roman Catholic secular institutes, of the Little Brothers of Jesus, the Community of the White Stone or of the Italian Focularini. We should not single these out if we did not see in them something we regard as exemplary. There are many different ways of looking at the various communities that have come into existence spontaneously and independently of each other in many parts of the world Church. Their development might properly be described as a community movement. All its parts share *one* particularly significant characteristic: their tendency away from the structures of the established churches towards life in communion with their unchurched fellow men. *Simple présence.*

These widely differing experiments, some of them most problematic, these attempts to revive and romanticize the past are in harmony with each other in not constituting withdrawal but an attempt to penetrate the world. They do not stand aside from events or set themselves apart, but seek to be responsible for the everyday events of life. These communities are not blueprints but experiments, not models but pointers to possible answers. They insist on interior contemplation for the sake of participation in real life. They are at one and the same time protests against the false worldliness and against the false other-worldliness of the Church. They are the result of the rediscovery of the unity of prayer and action, of sacrament and reality, of worship and service.

Migration to Real Life

The boldest experiment in identification has been that of the French worker priests. The change that came upon this group of clergy when they put away their cassocks and immersed themselves in the working world of the proletariat was so radical and unexpected that they inevitably found themselves in conflict with their church, a conflict which came as a shock. These men did not see themselves as spiritual emissaries of a religious organization leaving the security of the church for enemy territory in order there to give pastoral care to the alienated. In fact they had, as priests, become workers who shared totally in the way of life and working conditions of their fellow-workers. They had become *men without privileges*. They discovered that their hope of converting the workers to the Church was reversed; it is they who went through a process of radical alienation from the Church.

Mission must involve the readiness to jettison customs and traditions that have hitherto been thought essential. Mission is total self-giving. It is a departure with no hope of return. In history, mission has often demanded a cutting loose from the Church. There are occasions on which, if one is to be at the place demanded of a Christian, alongside one's fellow-men, one must leave the Church as one might leave father and mother, to whom one owes no less than existence itself. The extent to which a mother is capable of letting her children go, is the measure of her motherhood. *Faithfulness to the Church is realized in letting go of it, rather than in holding fast.* This lies in the Church's very nature, it becomes the Church by giving itself up. It is bidden to be expendable. Its appropriateness lies in its own disappropriation. Instead of cultivating its own religious environment the Church, in apostolic freedom, should live in an alien, irreligious world, being at home where it is not at home. There is no such thing as the world of the Church but only a Church of the world. *The Church is no more recognizable than the God who emptied himself.*

'You have no idea,' we read in one of the letters of the

worker-priest Henri Perrin, 'what it means to be a Christian outside the Christian ghetto with all its busyness, its traditional false questions and—there is no getting away from it—its betrayal . . . I feel the need to immerse myself ever more deeply in life at its poorest and most common; to get to know this world, to belong to it, to be one with it in order to find redemptive purpose at its heart.'

Just that is the point of the faith today. It may once have been right to *emigrate* on the 'negative' way (*via negativa*) from an unchristian world in order to attain holiness. Today, Christians are called to *immigrate* into the world of secular everyday affairs. The call for 'lay involvement' that is heard today in all the churches is an expression of this need. It is generally too superficially interpreted as a mere liberation from clerical control or as an encouragement to laymen to take up new duties in the Church. What is really needed is a Church that is present in and identifiable with the day-to-day realities of life. This call to establish communication between Christians and non-Christians is concerned with no less than the essential apostolate of the Church in the world.

The layman does not represent the Church, he is the Church. It is not just that he has a personal interest in salvation. He is the instrument of salvation. He is called to fulfil the Church's mission to the world. He must be proof that the Church and its theology is directed worldwards. Among laymen a dialogue takes place without which the Church fails to become Church, theology fails to become theology and the world fails to

95

become world. It is in the layman's breast that both the world and the holy scripture confront each other and strive to be understood.

The 'discovery' of the laity is most certainly not merely a ploy for taking some of the burden from the shoulders of the clergy. Were that the case it would only serve to confirm the clerical establishment. On the other hand there is no question either of the abolition of the clergy. Yet there is no escaping the fact that the clergy are hardly likely to emerge unscathed from this process of change, the more so as the exercise of the ordained ministry becomes ever more open to objection and ever more depressing as its complete inability to cope with the contemporary situation emerges. In tomorrow's Church and society the status and function of the ministry is likely to undergo vast transformation. In the future structure of the Church the clergy will need to play a new role, caught up in the economy of God's saving acts in the world, with the Church equipped as a charismatic and serving instrument. The laity, the people of God, include the clergy and embrace the whole Church. The lay movement does not aim at an elimination of the different functions and talents now in existence but at the long overdue removal of false distinctions between the ordained and the unordained. The solidarity of Christ with humanity establishes a completely new relationship between God and the world, one in which the contradiction between the sacred and the profane is eliminated. It is the function of the laity to exemplify Christ's solidarity with the world. To demand this type of involvement from the laity is simply to expect the Church to be the Church.

Our age provides the Church with the opportunity to discover its own nature. It is true that Luther too proclaimed the priesthood of all believers. What he in fact left us with, as Eugen Rosenstock-Huessy has pointed out, is a priesthood of all theologians. In fact Karl Marx's unkind sally that Luther could well afford to turn the priest into a layman because he had succeeded in turning the layman into a parson is not far wide of the mark. Traditional lay piety was wholly derived from that of the clerics. The call to the Church to be a lay community of Samaritans, not of priests and levites, has only now become impelling.

Secularization is only deepening a crisis within the Church that the Gospel itself brings upon an institution that has established itself as a purveyor of a particular type of culture, as a religious court of appeal and as a dispenser of salvation. In theology since Paul, the Apostle of the Gentiles, who has never failed to shock the pious of all traditions, the duality between what is regarded as spiritual and as worldly has always been called in question, but never wholly eliminated. Only a world that has gone totally secular has been able to rob this duality of all significance. It is because of this that today's Church is in the process of being reduced to its essence. It is being called upon to make true that essence in lay and not in clerical terms. The discovery of the Church's nature as a lay body is revolutionary in the sense that the New Testament is revolutionary. Yet that

necessary revolution has so far been side-tracked into
the safe waters of religious order. That is just as true of
Protestantism—albeit in slightly less obvious form—
as of Catholicism.

The future of the Church will depend on whether it
can produce the sort of people who demonstrate in their
lives what Christ's identification with the world is like,
people who will share fully in the world's life without
sacraments or other forms of security on which to fall
back, people caught up in the crowd, willing to speak
and to listen without prejudice, without knowing better,
people sharing in the thought of others, in their suffering, making decisions with them, sharing their hopes;
being *present* wherever men think, choose, suffer and
hope. That is why in our ecumenical jargon the *fraternal
worker* replaces the paid conversion-agent. The fraternal
worker stands alongside his non-Christian neighbour as
an equal who enjoys no privileges. The conscious moti-
vation of the ordained ministry virtually robs it of
missionary impact; the layman, on the other hand,
should make this impact because he has no ulterior
motive. Evangelization happens when the sons of God
enable others to share with them the new reality re-
leased by the Son of God. It does not happen at a
distance but when men converse, it is not done by
talking down to others from a pulpit, it happens in their
midst. It is comparable, as D. T. Niles has said, with
the moment in which one beggar tells another where
there is food to be had.

Our claims and declamations have ceased to matter.

What counts is our *presence as brothers*, brothers in an age described by many as the age of the *absence of God*. In fact it is not God that is absent but Christians. We can neither prove the absence of God nor establish his presence. We can only ensure our own presence and guarantee it. That is the very point of the alleged absence of God. He does not wish to be present, other than in us.

Faith has become strangely silent. Often it is better communicated in silence than in speech. Speech has been reduced to mere words, to no more than chatter. Our speaking is in an acute state of crisis. Our words no longer mean anything. What we say no longer convinces others, it merely labels us as a sham. In the very act of saying God, we have generally passed God by. Perhaps we shall have to go through a period of saying less in order to give our faith a chance to discover speech or to wait until our words begin to convey faith, truth, clarity, hope and to reveal the hidden, to articulate the hitherto unrecognized. Language only comes into its own when it is an expression of the very essence of life, when it gets to grips with life's utter secularity. It is only in this context that the words we speak can take on new significance. These words can only begin to convey faith if they do not take faith for granted *a priori*. The Church is in reality nothing, if it is not a vehicle of communication. This communication will get under way and will go on taking place if and *only* if we are prepared to share our life in true fellowship with other men. This is the work of evangelism, work which

99

today is not primarily that of one profession but of each one of us in our profession. We are called to represent Christ spontaneously and with incalculable consequences in the pedestrian obscurity of everyday life.

4

THE CHURCH IN A POST-RELIGIOUS AGE

The churches because they are products of their own historical development have also become their own enemies. I believe that wherever we show ourselves unwilling to cease being what we have become, history in the making will in its judgment strike us like lightning. That goes for each individual church-going Christian as well as for the institutions and customs of the churches. Despite our orthodoxy and regularity we have reached a dead end.

ALFRED DELP

Escape from the World, and into the World

WHEN the Church began its pilgrimage nineteen hundred years ago it consisted of scattered communities which had neither power nor wealth. Even though these communities were tiny minorities without statistical significance, they possessed the dynamism and effectiveness of a resistance movement totally committed to its cause. They changed the course of history, even though their actions brought persecution and suffering upon them. There is almost certainly no historical parallel for what they achieved. Indeed, we are still reaping the benefits of their achievement.

Anyone looking at the Church as it is today will hardly guess at such beginnings. Although, at any rate here in Germany, the Church enjoys almost limitless official patronage and can count on vast public support, it is beginning to take fright at its own impotence which contrasts strangely with its apparent prestige. The French Dominican Pie Duployé sums it up like this: 'The system works but its motor is idling in neutral.'

The parochial structures are impersonal and over-sized, they make impressive statistics, but serve to confirm society in its present form rather than to change it. They are more of a decoration than a provocation. The meeting-places of Christians have long ceased to be their dwellings or the hidden recesses of the catacombs. They now need cathedrals, impressive conference centres, olympic arenas and all that the mass media can offer. They are part of the structure of society with its clubs and associations. The churches have successfully helped to bring about a situation in which denominational allegiance and public patronage go hand in hand. Is it too much to say that the denominations have become 'protection rackets'? Heinrich Heine, as much as a century ago, described Baptism as the ticket to a better life. People need such tickets, such privileges, acquired by membership of a party, an association or a denomination and it can be a bitter pill to do without them. People are subjected to victimization, partly hidden, partly overt (sometimes in error described as clericalism) which the Church does nothing to prevent. On the contrary, the Church fosters it assiduously and must take its share of the blame for it.

Few people seriously suppose that the Church stands for anything or has anything to offer which society in its present form does not also accept and possess. Since the Church has abandoned the 'economy of faith', it has espoused the 'faith of the economists'. Our churches in Germany have made the inspector of taxes the arbiter of membership. The Church has fitted itself into the economy of society and in return for not upsetting any apple carts is paid as much as it wants. The Church is left with a good deal of room in which to manoeuvre. This is all too easily confused with freedom. The Church can even get away with preaching 'repentance'; it can go so far as to rouse applause when it calls on the nation to change its ways. In fact, were the Church to stop making such proclamations, society might be tempted to order their resumption. There is a need for this no less than the need for theological alibis to manufacture instruments of mass murder. Similarly the Church is required to give ideological cover for the traditional friend-foe-line-up which makes such moving emotive appeal at election times.

The Church is more inclined to conform than to protest. It appears in its present form to have deprived itself of the freedom to express dissent, of the vigour to attack the status quo, of the impartiality to criticize and of the resources to improve and to renew. Nor does the Church seem able to distinguish truth from falsehood or to be alive to creative possibilities. It is not that the Church is unwilling to do what it should or to leave undone what it should not do. It is simply incapable of doing it! Good intentions or their absence are not at issue; what is at issue is the very structure of the Church. Its ecclesiastical constitution no longer harmonizes with its spiritual purpose. The Church has become its own greatest enemy. Any critique which fails to take the magnitude of this dilemma into account is inadequate. Most such critiques content themselves with proposing that a clericalism of the left should supplant a clericalism of the right. In doing that they create a false antithesis.

To observe that the Church has been 'naturalized', has conformed with the world and has settled down to comfortable domesticity in it is only one side of the coin. Here now is the other. The Church is an integral part of society, yet at the same time a part that cannot be integrated. However much the Church merges naturally with its environment it remains apart, keeps its distance. The very act of belonging to the Church implies a certain alienation from the world, an alienation that cannot be shaken off.

If the Christian community was at one time a vanguard, it is today a rearguard. 'The light of the world' has now been reduced to its rear light. Divine service, the original purpose of which was mission (go forth!), has now been reduced to a retreat from the world. The Church has become a Gospel receiving set, quite forgetting in the process that it was created to be a transmitter.

No wonder then that Christian congregations go on existing as blameless, dull and unimaginative groups of people capable of surprising no one, at best supplementing life but never being its leaven, its very foundation. They exist on the periphery of people's lives like allotments on the edge of a big city. J. C. Hoekendijk likens all their activities to 'the churches' coastal shipping' or to 'spiritual suburban traffic'. A preacher who lives in a working class district of an English city has said in no uncertain terms that it is irresponsible to invite to church those whose way of life and thought is far removed from that of the local churches as they now are. The stranger would need to choose between feeling thoroughly ill at ease in church or radically changing his habits of life and thought; yet it is these that his new life as a Christian is supposed to enrich. To say this is simply to register what we know all too well: *real* life runs parallel to, unaffected by and unrelated to the Church's influence. The Church has developed a life of its own, more likely to deceive men than to uphold them, more given to self-justification than to mission, maybe still capable of feeding fish caught long ago, but certainly not equipped to go fishing. At times one is tempted, as was Georges Bernanos, to ask these churches: 'Just what have you done with grace?' We need to fly in the face of current formulations and traditions with a healthy portion of Christian disrespect—cheek, if you like—if we are to be free to think, to say and to do what currently needs doing. And what currently needs doing *is* the Gospel.

A sizeable collection of books already exists in the sphere of religious sociology all pointing to the paradox that, on the one hand, the Church has uncritically accepted the life and thought-patterns of secular society while, on the other, regarding itself as something special, becoming more and more introverted and from the outsider's point of view exclusive, unapproachable and inhospitable. So the Church is both conformist when it should not be and stand-offish where it should be involved. The Church becomes guilty at those very points where it fails to become unpopular. It hopelessly mixes up scandal and *skandalon*; in its attempt to avoid the former, it shirks its duty to *be* the latter, the conscience and therefore the constant irritant of society. It has shut itself up in a modern ghetto compounded of privilege and 'public relations'. Peter L. Berger in *The Noise of Solemn Assemblies* points out this paradox, the considerable social activity of the Church alongside its social irrelevance: 'On the one hand organized religion has a role to play in society. Without that role it could not play the role it actually does. On the other hand the forces that determine the shape of society are disinterested in organized religion, it in no way influences them and really makes no attempt to do so.'

Look closely, and you see that the Church's worldliness shows up its remoteness from the world. We have here once again the fact that this worldliness and its apparent opposite are really one and the same thing. Similarly, the clericalization of the Church and its 'spiritualization' are two sides of the one coin. This may, in its way, be justified and yet it might well be asked whether all this does not point to the Church's divorce from reality. A Church which has lost its grip on the world need not be surprised if the world gets on very well without it. A Church which makes no attempt to listen to what the world has to say corresponds to a world which is equally disinterested in the Church's message. This is the more true because a Church which is out of step with the world is almost certain to be out of step with its own purpose. Why then should anyone take much notice of it, why should it be thought to have anything worthwhile to say about the ultimate issues of life and death?

The liturgical year illustrates the point I am making. It is given great prominence in society (e.g. in radio and television programmes) but in reality it has long since ceased to have much meaning. Seen statistically and measured by the number of people who go to church, and looking at the non-religious significance of the Christian festivals, it is quite obvious that society's values are far removed from the liturgical orders of precedent. Although the early Church drew its power from Easter and Pentecost, the festivals of Christmas, Good Friday and All Souls as well as the Sunday dedicated to remembering the departed have in Germany become much more popular because they are part of social and personal experience. In other words those festivals that correspond to human experience because they are concerned with ordinary matters like birth and death are readily accepted. Not so the proclamation of resurrection, of ascension and of the outpouring of the Spirit which are thought to be unreal abstractions without analogy in life.

Perhaps the Church should have proclaimed the message of Christmas less ambiguously and in more uncompromisingly Christian terms; perhaps it should have spoken more realistically of the meaning of Easter. But that is beside the point. What needs to be recognized is that the Church's seasons have been picked up and given general significance and in the process have been torn from the context of their true background, overlaid with irrelevant significance.

The Church's year has been made to serve the strangest purposes. It is made to serve the purposes men want it to serve and not those inherent in its origins. This process of alienation in the course of which Christian festivals have become divorced from their true significance is not simply the work of the world. Its origin lies in the Church itself. In the past it either neglected to preach relevantly at the right time or it left the preaching to a few specialists.

The upshot is that we must face the fact that the Church's calendar is irrelevant to those outside it. The customs which go with each festival tend to obscure it rather than to reveal its meaning. They get between truth and men, and promote nothing but their own spurious glory. They are no more than showpieces pretending to conjure up something that was once tangible but now totally fail to convey its significance. They are incapable of establishing patterns of life that make sense in industrial society. All they seem to do is to try to fit everything into an ever recurring annual cycle whereas they should be proclaiming the news of what is to come.

Think of Christmas, done as it is to death. If Christmas means no more than most people take it to mean the world can well afford to be without it. There is no need to be an iconoclast to disapprove of the seasonal festivities and the host of more or less pagan customs that go with them. The Christmas glut of sickly sentimentality combined with an orgy of moneymaking by the business community can no longer even warm a child's heart. All the hectic activity merely seems to underline our monumental boredom. Everything confirms that no one expects anything of Christmas. The reasons may range from commonsense and honesty through disappointment to cynicism. Is this a lack of faith? Or have the Church's chickens merely come home to roost, the Church having failed to find words to make the Incarnation an event that gives our life true humanity because God became man?

Even more astonishing (at any rate in Germany) is the 'success' of Good Friday. This day takes its origin from the most alien, scandalous, unreasonable, unceremonious and irreligious chapter in the Bible. Good Friday should be the last day to satisfy the most disparate pious emotions whose origins are not easy to identify. There would have been some point in abandoning Good Friday, denying or not recognizing it. By such negative action men might have shown a better appreciation of its nature than by wrongly glorifying it, turning it into one of its great feasts and at the same time reducing it to generalities. Is this the way the Church innoculates itself against what happened on the Cross? Do the pious de-gut the faith by giving it an impressive religious framework, leaving God subject to the extremest of profanities, while they silently do away with him, be it on Calvary, in Auschwitz or in some other place? How can we square the aesthetic image of Good Friday, from Bach to Wagner, with him 'who had neither form nor beauty'? Is it possible to reflect the sobriety of the New Testament narrative by simply being sad on Good Friday and happy on Easter Sunday? Good Friday is often defended as though it were a last ditch, all that remains of sound tradition, a straw to clutch at in an age devoid of meaning. But is there really any difference between turning Good Friday into everyman's day of mourning and debasing the feast of Christ's birth into the German festival of *Weihnacht*?

The Church's year is tied to a way of life with which we are no longer familiar. It presupposes a link between the life of the Church and the life of the community which no longer exists. The more concrete and relevant it may once have been, the more useless and dated it now is. It has a past but no future. Martin Walser writes in his book *Halbzeit*: 'I inherited God in the traditions of the past and now I lose him on account of those very traditions.' For many of us these traditions can only be accepted at the cost of our integrity. Meanwhile the religious calendar goes on being acted out in its golden cage—and bit by bit it is killed in the process. It does nothing to serve the historical process which it presumably means to benefit. We have emptied it of relevance, of reality and of effectiveness.

Experiment in Freedom

Well then, is the Church to catch up with the times by adopting every new fashion? Or is its real task that of embodying the immutable when everything is in the process of change? In fact to regard the Church as a timeless entity is the gravest of misunderstandings. The Church has no normative validity *per se*; there is nothing inherently sacrosanct about it. It must always as a matter of principle be part of its own age. If in many respects the Church *is* more at home in the past than in the present, that does not prove its timelessness, quite the contrary. The Church becomes a period piece. The Church can only transcend time by reliably expressing its true nature in harmony with every age. Luther says that the Church is not a *being* but a *becoming*, not static but dynamic. The Church is not like a statue which is immune to the changes of history, surviving them unaltered, but is dynamically related to events, unable to be true to itself unless it faces what happened yesterday and what is likely to happen tomorrow in total commitment to the present moment. As the events which bring the Church into play are subject to an endless process of change, so must the Church be. Like Abraham it must always be prepared to emigrate from its accustomed dwelling places. We may take our bearings from the past, but only in order to master the future. He who

came, is he who will come. Tradition does not merely
live by that which was, but by him who will come. It is
the wind blowing into our sails, driving us forward. *The
only principle that can maintain the Church is its renewal.*

The Church is in no position to base itself on the
Incarnation if at the same time it attempts to justify the
immobility and untouchability of its institutions. My
criticism is not an attack on institutions as such. It is
turned against a static institution that becomes an end
in itself, that goes on functioning when it has become
irrelevant, that has no historical perspective and that in
the last resort is a perversion of true spirituality. The
relative is treated as though it were absolute. And at the
same time, it is not understood that absolute values can
only be recognized in the context of the relativities of
ordinary life. Christianity cannot be institutionalized
independently of the processes of history. The Church is
an experiment in freedom always on the move. It must
always be contemporary. An antiquated Church is not
merely a tragedy but an impossibility; it is no Church
at all. Those therefore who want the Church to remain
as it is are hardly likely to be its friends.

If the Church has the will to start serving those from
whom it has hitherto stood aloof it will need to stop
defending its present structure and begin to reshape and
diversify itself imaginatively and generously. Failing
that, it will never be all it should be to all men and will
continue to be of no more than little use to a few men.
As it is, the Church is reduced to a middle class institution, narrow-minded and stuffy. And so a totally mis-

leading image is created. We label as faith what is a mere expression of opinion. To many people this bourgeois code, this stuffy atmosphere, this blinkered outlook is unbearable. In consequence their relationship to the Gospel remains an open question. Their queries, expectations and hopes never come near to being taken seriously.

If they *were* to be taken seriously and given satisfying answers, there would need to be a Church with an open door and an open mind, a readiness to discuss issues and a totally new flexibility. The Church will only be capable of this if it produces free, loosely organized groups of people in community, people without privilege who will mainly be concerned with serving society anonymously in its varied structures into which they will need to be integrated. Meeting-places are needed, not organizations, people not committees, Christians in their profession and not professional Christians. Groups of people will be needed who are not part of a vast organization but are flexible and mobile, always ready to go into action, keeping up with events or even ahead of them, subtle enough to cope with the complexity of modern life and, for all these reasons, in a position to make a meaningful contribution to it. The Church would need to diversify its life and its work without limit in order to cope with the multiplicity of modern situations in town and country, both in public and in private life, if it intends to be present as salt and light. The Church needs to move to the places where people really are. If it does not, and goes on waiting for the people to come to it, the number of those who by habit and inclination accept active church membership is bound to diminish even further. Sooner or later the Church will then be reduced to a sect or a ghetto.

There will be no escaping the need to take a fresh look at our inadequate understanding of what community is about. An analysis of our attitudes which takes in dimensions of social psychology would reveal some interesting facts. As seen by the social historians Christianity, divided within itself, yet its ranks closed against the outside world, has been of dubious benefit to mankind. It is easy, without doing violence to the facts, to attribute communism to the failure of the Church to create a convincing Christian community. The exclusiveness of any group betrays the immaturity of its members, their infantile desire to be something apart, their demand for special treatment and their need for protection. There is more concern on their part for immunity than for community. Anyone not of their in-group is treated as a stranger. And it is not a far cry from the ostracism of the stranger to his defamation. The moment the Church takes on the traits of any such exclusiveness it ceases to be the Church, the true task of which is to lead men and societies into community and co-operation rather than into conflict.

Faith communicates. It has something to say which cannot be suppressed. And so, where there are Christians one expects fellowship to be born. This very fellowship, born of the communion that communication demands, cannot go on existing for its own benefit. It exists for the benefit of others. It was Bernanos who said that a Christian cannot be saved alone. This is equally true of the Christian community. As a matter of principle it cannot be a closed community. It must be open to all. This community is the fulfilment of the basic fact that man does not truly exist as a person unless he exists as a social being.

The Christian community will need to be ruthlessly de-romanticized and stripped of its irrationality. The Church will need to emerge from the twilight of its cultic existence into the clear and sober light of real life and its needs. Community is not a condition but an activity. It only comes to life 'in the act'. Only then is it truly apostolic. Such community lives by being an exchange of experience, a dialogue and, with it all, a prerequisite for effective action. If community seeks to preserve its own identity, it spells its own destruction. It is not an end in itself but finds its identity in the tasks which confront it and which, when fulfilled, enable it to go out of existence.

We live in an age which has been destructive of community and yet desperately searching for it, an age searching for people with a sense of belonging to each other, for team spirit, for dynamic minorities, for opportunities to share experience, for mutual encouragement, information and correction—oases in a wilderness. Hitler's gigantic machine was threatened more than anything else by the small groups who formed the resistance movement. We cannot fail to notice the lack of such responsible groupings both within the Church and outside it. The essence of life in dialogue is as little present in our blocks of flats as in our factories, in political life as among our intellectuals, in our laboratories as among journalists. Yet no important insight can be reached or decision made by an isolated individual; it requires the critical evaluation of all conceivable points of view. There is no simple and obvious way of making decisions, no way of totally grasping the implications of a situation; there is only the possibility of making the wisest conceivable choice. Every thought, every question, every decision, in fact everything of which we are aware has become highly complex. This state of affairs demands an exchange of minds, depends on open discussion, mutual inspiration and the constant corrective we must be to each other.

It goes without saying that the Church is not going to split up into scattered, disorganized groups. No doubt it will need to retain its structures and its administrative machinery, it will need to be one 'lobby' among others, it will need to remain a public body harmonizing with the legal requirements of a pluralistic society. It is bound to be one organization among others. But at the same time it should provide the ferment in every sphere of modern life. The people of God can only be effectively and convincingly present as missionary minorities in the countless different situations of modern life if they are prepared to work in teams which are subject to no anxious control, which work to no fixed pattern, which are in every sense unofficial and which sit loosely to the structures of our pluralistic society. All that will distinguish these 'teams' is the nature of their fraternal presence-in-the-world. These informal minorities will need to complement the established Churches, and will at the same time constitute a creative opposition to them. Church history has never lacked examples of such duality.

These small 'cells' still need to discover what forms they should take and explore the possibilities open to them. All that matters is that they should really find modes of existence true to their own nature and not alien, borrowed from history or clerical. The task in hand must alone determine the shape of the group setting out to tackle it. There will be no limit to the multiplicity and multifarious nature of these groups. They will stand in creative relationship with present realities, will learn from these and experiment in the light of them. They will not so much assimilate as integrate. Their solidarity will be anything but conformity. This solidarity embraces all things, all the elements of conflict and tension. Without conflict, solidarity becomes meaningless, new life cannot take shape. It is worth noting that all these developments have been taking place throughout the world Church and here and there have achieved significant results. Isolation is deadly. The more encouraging, then, that a network of friendship and common aspiration spans the globe keeping many people, however informally, in touch with each other. Those who have this sense of mutual belonging have as much right to describe themselves as the Church as the official bodies which so describe themselves.

The more effectively these groups are at work in the world, the better will they be equipped to do what badly needs doing: to restore reality to worship, to set it free from its Sunday isolation and to place it squarely where the New Testament means it to be, in everyday life. Worship should be a process of opening and not of closing doors. It ought not to be an endlessly repetitive attempt to 'reserve' the sacred, but should constitute active penetration and illumination of the profane. The concern of worship for the world should reflect God's concern for the world. Worship, so understood, would produce people who welcome the questions of the doubters, who have no religious pretences, who gladly do without privileges (spiritual or otherwise), people who prize friendship more highly than ideals. As yet there are hardly any signs of this sort of worship. Let it not be thought that it can be attained merely by supplanting the organ with jazz trumpets or the beautiful language of the sixteenth century with modern idiom. Alfons Rosenberg wrote of the Church in a post-Christian age that instead of being a 'communion of saints' it needs to consist of the 'saints of the community'. The Church is beginning to rediscover that it is based not on hierarchy but on brotherhood, that partnership and not paternalism is its hallmark. This discovery, if we act out its implications, is surely our response in Christian obedience to the challenges of an altogether new world.

The Church in a Post-religious Age

Christianity Incognito

It is not by accident that the Cistercian Abbot Joachim, who was born in Calabria in the mid-twelfth century and who founded the Abbey of San Giovanni di Fiore in the remote Sila mountains, is proving to be of particular interest today. He divided up human history into three 'salvation epochs'. According to Joachim's teaching the historical development of these epochs reflects the dynamism of the triune God, Father, Son and Spirit. Joachim speaks of our servant status under the Old Covenant, our status as children of God under the New and of our status as the friends of God in the epoch of the Holy Spirit. The epoch of the Son is that of a sacramental, priestly Church. The epoch of the Spirit, however, calls for no clerical or magisterial authority, only for the unauthorized authenticity of fully responsible men who will themselves be the Church in the world.

Joachim's symbolic divisions were more in the nature of poetry than of theology. They need to be treated accordingly. No one will want to cast them in a superficial historic mould. A linear progression is surely not what is meant. This was more in the nature of an attempt at definition. It would be absurd to describe the Trinity in terms of a procession in time, let alone to play off the three Persons against each other. It is not that we are concerned only with the Spirit. What is significant is the coherence of all three and that we are once more beginning to grasp the nature of the correspondence between all three Articles of the Creed. For all our reservations and the distinctions we would want to make, we need no occult sense to recognize the validity of Joachim's spirituality. Even Lessing conceded that the doctrine of the threefold age of the world might make some sense. And recently Karl Jaspers suggested that we should distinguish between pre-history, history and world-history. The last of the terms which he suggested should be applied only to the future when mankind would be faced with a situation demanding global solidarity. Such thinking is not without consequences for a Church which is in the process of discovering its universal role. This role cannot be measured quantitatively. Universality is not measured in statistics but in openness to the whole world. Because of this openness, the Gospel must be publicly presented to mankind. It is addressed to the *oikumene*, the whole wide world and not to a closed community. The practice of ecumenicity demands that the Church after two thousand years of its history should accomplish something utterly new, never hitherto experienced, something fitting the 'third age'.

What the theologians have always known has suddenly begun to confront the Church as an alarming fact: as the Church is the subject of one of the Articles of Faith, there is little that can significantly be said of it in terms of statistics. The number of Christians outside the organized structures of the Church, the so called churchless protestants, is steadily growing. They already constitute a sizeable part of society; their potential has yet to be recognized. They will make some of the most vital decisions for mankind's future, some of them of greatest political importance—and it would not be difficult to cite concrete examples. These latent Christians will set in train vital future developments. Condescendingly the Church has spoken of these people as fringe dwellers, likening itself to a city. The image will not wear. The living Church is surely itself always on the periphery where nothing can be taken for granted, never ensconced in safety amidst city walls. The fringe dwellers might well be Christ's true soldiers today.

Where do the frontiers run between what is Church and what is not? There are many Church members who are not Christians. On the other hand there are many Christians who do not belong to the Church. This phenomenon need give rise to no pentecostal optimism but it points to a structural change which should be accepted without reserve. Paul Tillich comes close to describing this state of affairs when he distinguishes between a latent and a manifest Church. The latent Church is very much in evidence all round us. 'It often seemed to me,' wrote Tillich, 'that the latent Church was more truly Church than the organized Church, because it was much less caught up in the Pharisaic belief that it "possessed" the truth.' This sort of thinking is not unbiblical, however unacceptable it might be to the churches.

In view of all this, Joachim di Fiore's vision of the Spiritual Church might lead us to a practical, sober recognition that the Church of the future will probably need to be much less manifest than hitherto. It will need to be a versatile structure playing its game to any rules if in its poverty of spirit it is to come anywhere near the riches of the triune God whom it seeks to reflect. The idea that the official local Church in all its narrowness should alone *be* the Church can no longer be maintained. It is not merely supplemented, it is also called in question by all the other possible forms of the Church. Beside the parochial the Church must exist in non-parochial forms. While we can distinguish between the latent and the manifest Church we cannot draw a dividing line between them. Christianity needs both. In previous centuries the Church was thought to be the manifestation of God. Today, although we are unready for it and disturbed by it, we are confronted with a latent God. We cannot objectively tie him down. *The latent Church is nothing but the expression of a latent God.*

The future Church will not be a closed institution, sheltered and secure, but one that is open, designed to address itself to all men. With its past position of social security eroded, it will need to fall back in the most literal sense on its 'interest' in the whole world—its being *among men*. It will be challenged to abandon its ineffective official stance and to enter upon its true task of being effectively present *incognito*. Its life will be full of surprises, dispersed, unadministrable, endangered, full of risks; it will need to be mobile, never taking itself for granted and yet filled with greater responsibility and greater enthusiasm than ever before. There is no better way of describing it than as the salt of the earth. The food we eat is improved by salt. The salt is lost in that food. It is never restored to its original condition. It becomes part of other substances. It is scattered and dispersed beyond recognition. And yet it is essential.

The Church will go its way unknown, a stranger. Its hallmark may well be to go unrecognized in the world.